DOING TIME
EIGHT HOURS A DAY

DOING TIME
EIGHT HOURS A DAY

Memoirs of a Correctional Officer

JAMES R. PALMER

iUniverse LLC
Bloomington

DOING TIME EIGHT HOURS A DAY
MEMOIRS OF A CORRECTIONAL OFFICER

iUniverse books may be ordered through booksellers or by contacting:

iUniverse LLC
1663 Liberty Drive
Bloomington, IN 47403
www.iuniverse.com
1-800-Authors (1-800-288-4677)

ISBN: 978-1-4917-1197-2 (sc)
ISBN: 978-1-4917-1199-6 (hc)
ISBN: 978-1-4917-1198-9 (e)

Library of Congress Control Number: 2013918990

Printed in the United States of America.

iUniverse rev. date: 10/19/2013

This book is dedicated with love to my wife, Donna, who has supported me in whatever I wanted to do. She put up with the late nights, the overtime, and the endless stories that have been told and retold over the years. Most she can probably tell now herself.

And to those who have contributed to this book, my friends and colleagues, thanks for your input, support, and contributions.

And to Cathy with her red ink pen!

Contents

Glossary

AA/NA	Alcoholics Anonymous/Narcotics Anonymous
AKA	Also Known As; Alias
CPR	Cardiopulmonary Resuscitation
CTO	Classification and Treatment Officer
	Nonuniform staff known as the case worker. Was the inmates' go-to staff person.
DOC	Department of Corrections
DW	Deputy Warden(s)
	Most prisons had one or two. LLCC had two: one in charge of security and one for program staff and programs.
FISH	Fish Guard, New Officer
IA	Internal Affairs
	Dealt with internal security issues and investigations.
KCIW	Kentucky Correctional Institute for Women
KCPC	Kentucky Correctional Psychiatric Center
KSP	Kentucky State Penitentiary
	Kentucky State Police
LLCC	Luther Luckett Correctional Complex
OJT	On-the-Job Training

PO	Probation/Parole Officer
PC	Protective Custody
SMU	Special Management Unit, The Hole, Dodge City, Big House, Lockup, Seg, Solitary

The prison in a prison for housing the more violent inmates, or those seeking PC, or those convicted of a write-up or pending some type of disciplinary action.

SOTP	Sex Offender Treatment Program
TAD	Transportation Admission and Discharge

All inmates arrived and departed here for court, medical trips, new arrivals, etc.

UA	Unit Administrator

Non uniform staff. Senior nonsecurity staff in the dorms. The CTOs worked for him or her

Common Signals and Codes

While many different signals and codes are used in prison, just as they are in law enforcement, all agencies are working on eliminating their use in favor of clear text. That means plain speak, in case there are outside agencies involved. It's also easier to communicate, as sometimes in the heat of the situation, one can forget or mention a wrong code or signal code. A lot happens when the adrenaline is pumping and you are responding to a situation or an emergency and many things are happening all at once.

Radio Codes		Signal Codes	
1-1	Receiving poorly	Sig 1	At home
1-2	Receiving well	Sig 2	Meet me
10-4	OK	Sig 3	You have messages
10-5	Please relay	Sig 4	Go to office
10-6	I'm busy	Sig 5	Break
10-7	Out of service	Sig 6	Call me
10-8	In service	Sig 7	Staff needs help
10-14	Escorting	Sig 8	Disregard—Cancel
10-15	Prisoner in custody	Sig 9	Inmate fight—Disturbance
10-20	Your location	Sig 10	Medical emergency

10-36 Time, please

10-97 Arrived at . . .

10-98 Done with my last
    assignment

With all these to remember, you can see why almost all agencies are going to clear text or talk. Yes, the inmates can also hear and understand, but time is of the essence in any emergency. Your life could depend on it!

Disclaimer

All names have been changed to protect the identities of the staff and inmates still at LLCC or other state prisons. Many areas cannot be described in detail due to their sensitive nature and for security reasons.

Introduction

This book was written for several reasons.

Not knowing what transpired inside a prison led me to seek employment there—as compared to what we all see on television. I wanted to know what happens, as I always had a penchant for law enforcement.

Going into corrections fulfilled a personal urge, but I wanted to let the public in on what happens behind the concertina-wired fences, locked doors, and drably painted walls of a prison.

Follow the stories of officers and inmates on their daily journeys of trials and tribulations. Read how friendships are formed among the opposite sides and how they impact each other's lives.

And hopefully to prevent just one more person from going to prison.

The DOC (Mock) Miranda

You have the right to swing first. However, if you

choose to swing first, any move you make can and will

be used as an excuse to beat the shit out of you.

You have the right to have a doctor and a priest present.

If you cannot afford a doctor or are not presently attending

a church of your choice, one will be appointed to you.

Do you understand what I just told you, asshole?

This is a joke version of the actual Miranda warning, for our amusement and use only. It was not intended to replace the original Miranda warning.

Chapter 1

FIRST IMPRESSION

Box One is the first contact anyone has with the prison.

Be it staff, inmate, visitor, vendor, or police, they all must stop and check in at this post. Each visitor is asked if he or she has any drugs, alcohol, or weapons. Police and law enforcement officials secure their weapons here. Private citizens and visitors, even with concealed carry permits, are not permitted to bring guns on the premises. There are many signs posted prohibiting these and other items, and saying that all vehicles are subject to search.

If any contraband is found, the person carrying it is denied access to the grounds for that day. Occasionally, random searches are conducted by the prison SRT team. If and when *any* contraband items are found, the local police or state police are called and the carriers are subsequently arrested. Their visitation rights are either suspended or completely denied for up to a year. Even then, the person must apply to the warden for permission to visit.

Even when police come in to drop off or pick up prisoners, their vehicles are searched, because of all the weapons they carry: rifles, pistols, ammo, and tear gas or pepper sprays. All weapons must all be checked in and secured at this post.

As the many visitors arrive, they are asked if they have any of the above-mentioned prohibited items. Their response is usually the same: no. Some are spot-checked just to be sure. The volume of traffic on weekends and holidays is high, and a lot of cars come in bringing visitors.

In addition to checking all vehicles, prison guards check all visitors visually to make sure they conform to the dress code, which they all received a copy of at some time during their loved one's first week of incarceration. This is just a visual check, as they will be more thoroughly checked by the front desk officer.

After all, it is a men's prison. No tank tops, no bare midriffs, no showing of cleavage, no short shorts, and no short skirts. Shorts and skirts cannot be higher than six inches above the knee, and if it's close, it's measured. If it does not comply, the visitor is denied access until he or she complies. Many who are denied access use the local big box store to buy clothes that comply.

All commercial trucks are given the same checks when entering. However, upon departure, they are scrutinized more closely because inmates unload the vehicles and the potential for escape is greater, even though the trucks are checked at least two times before they get to the front gate.

Chapter 2

FIRST DAY IN PRISON

My Old Kentucky home, where the sun shines bright, as the song goes, except for today.

It was a typical cold, rainy spring day in Kentucky. The temperature was in the low 40s, a slight fog hung in the air like a horror movie in a cemetery, except it was daytime. The drizzle was steady. All in all, it was a miserable day to be outside, one that you would rather spend indoors keeping warm. But not here.

This was to be a very different day for me and the three others who had just been hired. We were on the way to becoming correctional officers, or prison guards, as we are sometimes called. And those are among the good terms we heard from the inmates.

But for now, we were on our way to pick up our uniforms and equipment. The uniforms includes hats, belts, jackets, and raincoats—if they had your size. We were also given a couple of blue jumpsuits. Some were new, most used, and all faded blue. (Hmm . . . the big blue line). And in spite of the manufacturer's tag, one size fits nobody. We all looked and felt like we belonged on a trash pickup crew or a garbage truck. We were also issued belts to hang our equipment on: radio pouches, first aid kit carrier, a pouch for rubber/latex gloves, and a mouth piece for CPR in the event we had to use it.

Leaving the warehouse, our arms full of our new gear, we proceeded to a car used to transport prisoners. Stowing our gear in the trunk, the four of us got in the car. This was our first (unless someone had been previously arrested or detained) experience with a car with doors that only opened from the outside, and a screen or partition separating the front and back seats. This was for the protection of the officers when transporting prisoners. Oh what joy, with the four of us in cramped in the confines of that smelly car!

I guess I knew what was coming next so I hustled to the passenger side of the car and got the front seat—shotgun, as it's called. I didn't want to be enclosed like sardines with the three of them, especially since one was rather rotund.

The first thing we noticed was it sure didn't smell like our cars. It reeked of the many prisoners who had been transported over the years. In the confines of a prison not everyone practices daily hygiene, so body odor can become a problem. Stale cigarette smoke, before the state banned smoking in state vehicles, body odors, funk and farts, stinky feet, all in an enclosed area. It was a smell we would all become to familiar with in the dorms.

Our trainer explained we were going to take a tour of the outside of the facility. We called him Lieutenant "I'm so cool I know it all," AKA Herman the German, and we would be reminded why we chose those nicknames on more than one occasion, even after training was over. He *never* let anyone forget it, either.

As we drove around the perimeter of the prison, the only constant beside the cold drizzly rain was the high chain-link fence with rows of razor wire attached to it on top and along the bottom. The razor wire is exactly that—razor sharp! Any one or any thing getting caught in it would be sliced and diced severely, like a Veg-o-Matic had gotten ahold of it. And the more you struggled, the worse it got. Severe slicing and entanglement—it could be real nasty. Occasionally a skunk or a raccoon would get caught in it. Nothing to do but wait and then have maintenance remove the carcass very carefully!

The DOC wanted to keep people either in or out but I don't know of anyone ever trying to break *into* prison. A lot of the convicts didn't want to be here, but some did; they got free medical care because they had no one on the outside to take care of them.

There were occasional signs that stated: **CAUTION. STAY AWAY / OFF THE FENCE. DEADLY FORCE IN USE!**

Very bold and intimidating if you're seeing it for the first time.

As we drove, the L.T. explained things to us, things we would later learn in more detail, about the yards, dorms, rehab programs, and recreation field. I was thinking to myself it was such a nasty day nobody would be outside. But I was wrong.

At the far end of the recreation field, I noticed many prisoners, or inmates, lifting weights and doing push-ups, generally working out in pairs, one lifting and one acting as a spotter.

I asked, "Isn't it too cold for them to do that?"

The L.T. snickered and said in his "I know it all voice," "It's never too cold for these guys. They are out here every day, rain or shine, cold, hot, windy, you name it. It's what they have to do all day every day. These are the serious guys who are the muscle of the yard. Most of them run everything that happens on the yard, the gambling, the betting, the "hits" (beat downs) drug running, (yes there are *a lot* of drugs in prison most brought in by staff), the scams, and just general mayhem."

My thoughts were that I was in decent shape, having served twenty-plus years in the military, but a few pounds heavier and a few steps slower, things that later would make it evident that I was indeed getting older and slower. Father Time kickin' my ass!

One of the comments from someone in our group was, "Oh shit, I guess it's true what we see on TV."

The lieutenant just laughed.

Driving around the perimeter, he told us, "Don't drive on the grass; watch the holes in the road; never drive the same pattern, because the inmates are always watching to learn our patterns and habits; look for holes in the fence, and check (shake) the fence in different random areas when doing fence checks. Just remember they are always watching you and tracking your every move, looking for your vulnerable spots."

The tour of the outside road complete, we then were shown the weapons we would be using on several of the different posts, such as perimeter post (driving around the prison in a state car), observation towers, Box One (entry and exiting the prison property), dorm control officer, dorm floor officer, and the various other program posts.

And the ever present and important post orders.

Post orders are the documents you are supposed to read when assuming a post. Each one is different for each specific post, and we would be required to learn them all in detail. They included what you should do in case of emergency, what to look for in different areas, and what you were required to do on that post. They had to be signed by each officer on each shift every day. After a while no one read them, they just signed them.

Now we began our "work" days in the prison, until the academy started in three days, walking around out here with our trainer/escort, observing, visiting all areas, always watching, observing, and asking questions. Learning the difference between inmates and convicts was another part of our indoctrination.

Inmates are the older guys who have been around for years. They know they are there for a certain period of time, their hell-raising time is done, and now they just want to do their time, be left alone, and try not to get caught up in the yard bullshit; i.e., gambling, making book, trading food for whatever. Convicts are the younger ones, the ones with a chip on their shoulders. They don't care, they don't want a job, and they are usually gang bangers with the saggy britches, an attitude, and the feeling that the whole world owes them something, everything. They can't be told what to do or be given any direction. They are pissed off at the world, pissed off at being here, and acting like *we* put them there. They are the first to say, "I'm not guilty. I didn't do it. They all lied on me."

There is a difference between the ones in prison and the ones in jail. In jail, your sentence is 365 days or less. In prison, your sentence is 366 days or longer. Months, years, decades . . . life. Or as the inmates called it . . . *forever.*

Chapter 3

Learning the Basics

Our new careers were now beginning to take some shape. All new hires for all the prisons are required to attend the academy. Here, we would learn daily activities such as post orders, daily logs, report writing, how to do cell searches, strip searches (not just get naked), procedures that would or could save our lives, powers of observation, and CPR in case we needed to use it on staff or inmates (Yes, I did), on an inmate.

Post Orders

These cannot be gone to in detail, as they are sensitive in nature. These are the orders that explain things for each post, things you *must* do—procedures to follow, who to notify in case of emergency, time schedules for opening and closing the dorms, and when to open and lock the outside gates that surround each dorm.

They are brief and to the point. Post orders must be signed and dated every day on each shift, by each officer.

Daily Logs

These are the logs kept on each post of who worked that post on any given day, who relieved whom for breaks, and what happened during that shift. Hopefully it was a quiet day and nothing happened. All staff and inmates who enter the dorms had to be documented with the time they entered and left.

This information could be useful later if someone accused an inmate of being in a restricted area (not his dorm) or if someone needed to prove where he was at a particular time.

All cell searches had to be recorded. We had to remember that all the paperwork we did was legal documentation and subject to be subpoenaed for any court proceedings.

Logs had to be complete and accurate.

Cell Searches
Glove up.

Wear rubber gloves. This was for our protection. Take nothing home to your family!

Cell searches were done on a random basis and logged in the daily log so as not to pick on any particular inmate. They were also done if you suspected something illegal in the cell. We were taught to be systematic in doing these searches. First, the inmates had to be present, either one or both. Second, we were taught to pick a start point, third, be thorough and consistent in going around the cell, fourth, start in one corner and work your way up and down and go around. Check on, in, and under things. Dump out boxes of soap powder and cereal (great places to hide things because few officers look), into bowls or other containers, but be neat and try to keep things as sterile as possible—respect went both ways. Or have the inmate dump it out as you watch. Put it in bowls or other containers. Check in between pages of books, in the bindings of books—nice spot for razor blades and tobacco. Inmates' hiding places were ingenious. After all, they had twenty-four hours a day to think about these things. We had eight hours, minus lunch of thirty minutes, to find things. Quite lopsided!

When checking under ledges, we didn't just run our hands along the edges. Those were a favorite hiding place for the inmates to put razor blades, and running our hands across them led to serious cuts with a dirty, used razor blade that was probably contaminated. We felt, touched, patted or used a mirror to help us. I carried two mirrors with me, a dental size for small, tight places and a two by three inch for general areas, such as under the rims of toilets, behind pipes, under garbage can lids, under door frames, and other hard to reach places.

Strip Searches

We were taught to use discretion when performing these. Before doing a strip search, you had to have great suspicion of someone hiding something on or in their person to do this, and then a supervisor had to be notified as to whom, what you were looking for, and what your suspicions were. And always keep your eyes on the person in question. Some of the prisoners were outstandingly quick at sleight of hand. Practice, practice, practice. The only exception to this rule is visits. We were required to strip search all inmates on their way back to the dorm after a visit, and to keep a log of all searches.

CPR—Cardio-pulmonary resuscitation.

We all had to learn this in case we needed to perform CPR on another staff member or an inmate. This was also good to know in case you needed it at an accident scene or for a family or friend at home.

We were all issued a CPR mask in the event we needed to perform the rescue procedure. After all, it is mouth to mouth.

Disciplinary reports

Also known as write-ups, these were done when an inmate violated the rules. Generally reserved for the more serious rule infractions, they could also be used for such trivial things as littering (throwing a match on the ground), spitting on the sidewalk (it spreads disease), and not making your bed. But it was a good tool since the inmates hated getting them because they could cause a black mark on an inmate's record if or when they went before the parole board. They could affect his dorm assignment, or getting a better job. If serious enough, the write-up could also cause loss of good time (time earned toward reducing their sentences) or put them in segregation.

When writing these reports, we were taught to keep it simple, following the five w's and an h—who, what, when, where, why, and how. Follow that format and life would be good.

If you didn't, you'd have to rewrite it. We were also taught that after you write your report, have someone else read it before you turn it in. See if it makes sense and contains all the elements needed. These write-ups were then heard by a hearing officer, a supervisor, lieutenant or higher. The inmate was afforded all his constitutional rights and was even given a legal advisor, another inmate, whose job it was to provide legal counsel and assistance to him.

The write ups then became part of his permanent record unless dismissed.

Radio Operation

We were also taught simple radio operation. Some people had never used one so it was basic operations so we would all be able to use codes that could be and would be used in life saving situations—ours and theirs—to ask for breaks, advise supervisors of locations and situations, and call for assistance when needed. Basic communication.

After all, we were there to serve the public, protect the inmates from themselves and others, and watch over them as they did their time, not to mete out punishment, as this had already done by a jury of their peers.

Our academy class consisted of about thirty-eight officers, male and female. We came from all institutions across the state for our basic academy of six weeks training. (It was later changed to eight weeks). Some were new to corrections, some had previous experience, and some were returning after trying different job choices. After graduation, we would all return to our specific institutions to begin our OJT status for a period of six weeks, with two weeks on each shift—7:30 a.m.-3:30 p.m.; 3:30-11:30 p.m.; 11:30 p.m.-7:30 a.m. After this six-week period, we took an OJT test and if we passed, we were officially officers out on our own, assigned to different shifts and posts to fend for ourselves with the help of our partners.

Upon graduation, we were told: "Welcome to the Department of Corrections and the prison system."

Unfortunately, through the observation of the old-timers, we learned that the details we were taught to follow and told were important would become mere formalities we followed on each post we were assigned. As we would later learn, once we assumed our posts, reading everything on the logs was a luxury for which we had little time. Speed-reading became an important new skill.

As we truly learned the posts, we learned to pick out what we needed for the safety of ourselves, the facility, and the inmates.

Chapter 4

Welcome to a Different World

"Welcome to the Department of Corrections and the prison system."

That's what we were told when we graduated from the Academy. Now we were going to find out many things they never told us that were not in the books—but these were the things we would need to know to do our jobs.

Upon entering the prison we were treated like . . . common criminals. Imagine that.

At the front desk post, the officer in charge had everyone who entered—including us—go through the same routine: remove your jacket, empty your pockets, and put everything in plastic bowls, just like at an airport. Then that officer would look through your carry-in items, and your lunch bag, briefcase, and jacket went through the x-ray machine. There was a long list of prohibited items, such as tape recorders, pocket knives, cameras, and large amounts of cash, (over twenty dollars). Why would you need cash in a prison anyway? Any medications had to be in the original container and then only enough for two shifts, in case you had to work overtime. And if they were narcotics, they had to be left in the captain's office, and you had to go there if and when you needed to take a dose.

After getting all that checked and through the x-ray machine, we had to walk through a metal detector. Any keys, change, cigarette lighters, or belt buckles that were not put in the bowl would set off the alarm, and you had to start the process all over again. After clearing the front desk area, it was on to the roll-call room.

We had to go through the doors with signs that read, "Caution! Electric doors," which meant they were all controlled electronically by an officer who was monitoring them and you. The first door opened. You walked in, and it closed. **SLAM**!

Now you were in between two electronically controlled doors. One door couldn't open till the other closed. Then the second door opened and you were *inside* the prison.

Wow. We were inundated with strange new sights, sounds, and smells that were foreign to us. It was a while before we could differentiate what each one was.

When those doors slammed shut, it sent shivers up your spine. Just knowing you did not control the door was scary. And now it was hurry up and wait, wait for someone else to open the door or close the door. It was especially trying during an emergency. I often wondered how much time a person waited at the doors during a career in corrections. You think of the most mundane things while waiting for the doors to open. There were a few officers who, when that first door slammed shut, literally got the shakes and asked to leave. Maybe they couldn't take the confinement or not knowing what was going to happen next, or knowing they did not control the doors. Those officers generally resigned the same day. Better now than later if and when the shit ever hit the fan. And it always did. It was always just a matter of time.

Chapter 5

OFFICERS—GOOD AND BAD

Every organization had its good and not so good people. This is also true in the Department of Corrections. I learned this early on while still on OJT status. OJT was a time to learn, to watch, observe, to ask questions, to take notes, and to keep your mouth shut (my very weakness) and not make any comments. After all, we were just learning. I was reminded of this quite often.

We learned we shouldn't rock the boat—yet—because we were still "fish guards" (new officers), an endearing term often used by convicts and fellow officers. This stayed with us until we got off OJT status, and the next group came in. And that was not often enough—always a staff shortage.

The good officers, wanted to see us succeed and stay. It made for great camaraderie, smoother working conditions among those in whom you placed your trust, and it lowered the forced overtime, which everyone hated, not only because it usually came with no notice. The turnover in the DOC was horrendous for many reasons—low pay, long hours, forced overtime, and favoritism, for example. And the prisons operated 24 hours a day, 7 days a week, 365 days a year. Nights, holidays, and weekends, and in all types of weather. There are no holiday breaks in prison.

It took a certain minimum number of people to run a shift. If an officer couldn't get time off, he/she did the next best thing . . . called in sick. People, especially the officers with the kids, frequently used this trick to get days or holidays off. Me, I chose rather do my shift *on* the holidays, comp time and a half, versus money at time and a half, and build up my comp time to use when I wanted off. Build it up, keep it up, and stay close to the max of 230 hours. It worked all the time. The state and the institution had the rules, and the good officers learned to play their games well. I became a master of it. I was there twelve years and never put in a vacation slip. I let my maxed-out comp time get me time off when I wanted it. I kept my comp time and sick time to the maximum allowed. This would come in handy several times in my career. I had several major surgeries and took a lot of time off, but it was always with pay. And I still kept my time up.

Some officers didn't keep up, and when they needed time off, they didn't have it and had to ask others to donate time to them. Some gave; some didn't, because they *were* abusers. Those who were abusers didn't get much donated and consequently had to take time off without pay.

There were plenty of good officers. They came in, minded their own business, and did their jobs. They had the respect of the other officers and some inmates alike. They wanted to do their jobs, be professional, and go home safe.

Then there were the other ones.

One of my earliest recollections was of an officer, who was referred to as "Two-Liter" by other officers because he always brought a two-liter of soda to work.

When he worked the unit dorms, he would stay in the control center for a full seven and a half hour shift. Didn't even want a break for dinner. It took me several shifts to find out this soda bottle not only contained soda, but an alcoholic mixer as well. When I reported this to a supervisor, he said, "Okay, I'll look into it" . . . but little did I know that they were drinking buddies off duty and once upon a time had shared an apartment together. It took me a long time to find out that the supervisor told "Two-Liter" who had reported him. Strangely, I never worked that dorm again with that officer on that shift. This incident made me wonder who I could trust.

The DOC had a zero tolerance policy to *any* alcohol, so even the smell of it was a no-no. Two-Liter always came to work sober and smelling clean, but nobody ever checked him going home. Who would have thought it?

And while it was rare, there was an instance where an officer developed a homosexual relationship with an inmate. When the inmate made parole, the officer resigned, and they continued their relationship. The inmate later died of HIV related illnesses. I wonder if the ex-officer knew that.

There were also bad female officers. Some of them brought their problems on themselves, by thinking, "I could never fall for a convict." But the cons had all day and night to watch the officers, get the feel of anything wrong, and then engage them in conversation. They would use all sorts of lines on the women: Tell them they understood and knew how they felt; asked how things could be so bad for such a good person; told them their husbands or boyfriends just didn't understand them. The cons spent days thinking of what to say and when to say it, and some of the women longed to hear it.

So, after many long, lonely nights working in a dorm, being away at night, and hearing the cons' sob stories, or hearing what they didn't hear at home, the weak ones wore down. There was also the promise of love or money that sometimes became irresistible. And so they fell victim.

Many a female officer (and male officers, for different reasons) succumbed to bringing in contraband. We were always told never give anything to an inmate. The inmate's always watching you and learning how to con you. It usually started with something small, like, "Can I borrow your ink pen?" Or, "Can I have a light for my cigarette, I'm out of matches." "Boy, those cookies look good. Can I have one? It's been *forever* since I had a homemade cookie." And once you gave in they had you.

The next time it was something just a little bigger, until you were hooked. If you refused, they would casually bring up the fact "you gave me this or that and *we* saw you." There was always an accomplice watching the whole thing. (For reference, a good book to read is *Downing a Duck*). And then it got to the point where they demanded that you bring in dope. Sometimes they sweetened the pot (pun intended) by telling you how much money could be made and how easy it would be. The money would come from outside sources, sent to a post office box, or you would be met discreetly somewhere outside of prison. Money and dope would change hands and the deed was done. Dope was the major item smuggled in.

But you have to remember that if one person knew something, he's was going to tell someone, and it was usually his roommate. And then, because the only way two people can keep a secret is if one of them is dead, it began. Joe told Bob, who told Sam, who told Everett, etc., etc., and they all *swore* not to tell anybody. (See, where this is going . . . nobody can keep a secret). The story then eventually worked its way back to IA. (Internal Affairs) either by a con looking for something, or maybe a bit of help with a write up, or help getting a better job, or dorm, or an officer from one of his snitches. Either way, it's a long process to check out and investigate.

Then there is the story of Officer Stinky. He was a *veteran* of close to twenty years. He worked at the "girlie" prison (KCIW) and was promoted to sergeant. But that was short-lived, and he was transferred to the men's prison. Rumor had it that he had done some inappropriate things while at the women's prison. Rumors . . . . hmmm.

But at the men's prison, his work was shady. He constantly came in a few minutes late every day, looking like he slept in his uniform. One day he was assigned to escort a prisoner on a funeral detail. This was where the inmate got to go to a funeral of a family member, once it has been approved by the DOC.

While on this detail, the officer got very familiar with the mother of the inmate, and soon he was calling and seeing her on the side. He was married at this time, and his wife worked at the same prison. Needless to say, he was caught when the mother told her son the inmate who she was seeing and talking to. The inmate told Officer Stinky's wife, who told IA, who investigated it, found it to be true, and fired him. His wife resigned several weeks later.

Officer Kevin also had close to twenty years. He had a decent post. He worked Monday through Friday and had weekends and holidays off, a job that a lot of officers wanted. He got caught up in the dope thing, only his issue was self-destruction. He started calling in sick, then just failed to show up. When he did show up, he was unkempt, unshaven, and just plain nasty. Then he stopped coming to work altogether. Vanished. Disappeared. Faded away. So did his career. Poof. Gone. Up in smoke. His drug of choice? Crack. The last anyone saw of him, he was delivering sandwiches for a local sandwich shop. Delivering to? His old workplace, the prison. And he didn't make a lot of tips there. Ah—the irony of it all.

After the investigations were complete, stings were often employed to catch the dirty officers. And when caught, they were confronted, arrested, and dressed in an orange jumpsuit, (just like regular inmates), handcuffed, and paraded up the walkway in front of all the officers and inmates. The word spread like wildfire and everyone wanted to see who it was. The inmates really got a big charge out of seeing an officer handcuffed and escorted out by the police.

Many careers have gone south because of greed. When inmates choose staff they thought they could get to bring stuff in, the hook was set. With offers of money, and sometimes big money, depending on the drug being smuggled in, it was tempting to the weak, especially if the officer was in financial trouble. Many officers with fifteen to twenty years' service got nothing after getting fired for smuggling in contraband. No retirement, no benefits, no respect. And I'm sure it was hard to explain to a loved one what you did or what you got fired and arrested for. Was it worth it?

There were even those that "fell in love" with inmates. What the inmates could give was something nobody could understand. We all guessed the female officers became involved because they heard what they wanted to hear. Some officers even got hooked up with other officers, ruining many a marriage. After all, they usually spent more time with their partner at work then their partner at home. Most of the ones who ended up getting tangled up with the inmates usually had troubles at home or a weak support system. That made them more vulnerable to the "sweet nothings" the inmates had to say. And they said it with such conviction.

One way an inmate worked at getting an officer to fall for him or her was to get acquainted with the officer. They took a long time to feel each out emotionally and one way to make sure it was for real was to have the inmate contact his people on the outside to send a money order for the amount specified to a PO box. The officer would get the money order, and when the officer returned to work, the favor (usually sexual) was rendered. These favors were usually done in the dorms, behind closed doors, in the janitor's closet, in the officer's floor office, in the chow hall between meals, anywhere "privacy" could be had for ten to twenty minutes without anyone being missed or interrupted.

This is a primary reason many say that women should not work in men's prisons, or men in women's prisons.

On the opposite end were the good officers, who helped new officers and wanted to see them excel. They gave tips and pointers that helped a newbie stay a step ahead of the convicts or that could save someone's life. I met one on the third shift during my OJT period. He was very instrumental in me staying there and learning things to keep me safe and to deal with various situations.

He was a very young looking officer with the nickname TA. He didn't play politics; he just did his job and wanted to go home safely. His wife was also an officer on another shift, and his father-in-law was a captain. His best tips were on how to conduct myself, act professionally, and treat all inmates like I would like to be treated if I were in here. Very good and sound advice. It saved my ass many times. Many officers and supervisors used the phrase "firm, fair, and consistent." This officer observed that rule and he was respected by everyone I talked to. He taught us that if we followed that one rule, we'd never have any problems. How true, because you had nothing to be questioned about. Be above reproach.

While the officers had many jokes and comments about the inmates, we were sure they had some about us, and we often talked about "what ifs" in a particular situation. The bigger "what if" was what would you do if you had to do CPR on an inmate? After all they were *inmates*. The standard joke answer was to blow on one them and step on his chest, but many an officer performed when they had to. I know I did.

I was working in 7B one day, doing a floor patrol, walking the floor, just observing and making my presence known. I walked past a cell and noticed an inmate who appeared to be asleep. I knew this guy and had talked to him many times in the past. He was older, about sixty-something years old, in poor health, and just serving his time.

He had a sentence of fifteen years to do and was almost half way through it. I stopped to watch him and noticed his chest going up and down to be sure he was breathing. He was okay, all was well. I left and continued my patrol. When I finished that floor, my gut instinct told me to go back and check on him again. I stopped at his cell door and again watched for the chest movements. However, this time there were none.

Immediately, all my training kicked in. I didn't even think about what needed to be done. I just did it. I grabbed my radio and called a Signal 10, and announced that I was beginning CPR at that time. All that training on the CPR dummies came back to me. *Check. Call. Care.*

Take precautions.

I put my latex gloves on, took out my breathing apparatus and inserted it, and started CPR. I *checked* his pulse on his neck. I *called* for assistance, and I applied *care*.

Since I was the only one on scene, it was up to me to do the rescue breathing and chest compressions. I had completed about three cycles when help arrived. It was the lieutenant on the yard.

I told him, "I'll breathe, you compress."

We continued, and on his first set of compressions, we both heard his breast bone crack. It was a sound I will never forget. The adrenaline runs high. We continued this cycle until medical arrived on the scene and they took over. They tried to intubate him and that failed too. After several minutes, with an ambulance on the way, medical wanted to call it—meaning that he had died. They waited till they got to the hospital, and a doctor officially called it. *Dead.*

Dying in prison created a lot of paperwork. He had died and it was officially reported when he was at the local hospital.

And anyone who says this doesn't get to you is lying. I tried my best but still second guessed myself: What if, maybe, could I have done something more? I was given support by another lieutenant who must have seen something because he asked if I was all right.

I said yeah, but he knew differently. He walked me to see the prison psychologist, and we talked for about thirty minutes. It *had* gotten to me. That man was probably the finest lieutenant I worked for and with—compassionate, caring, and always with a kind word to say. He knew his job and took no lip from inmates. Most importantly, he backed his officers. If you were wrong, he never embarrassed in front of others, but he took the time to point out your mistakes in private.

After the inmate's room was cleared and secured, IA had to investigate to be sure it was not crime scene. It was not, and life moved on.

To the many good officers who helped me through the years, thank you. We all learned something. From the good, we learned how we should conduct ourselves. Be compassionate when needed, listen when someone is talking, and be hard when needed. We made it and preserved. We did our time, did our job, and went home safely. And some of us retired.

To the few officers—and I use that term loosely—who didn't, I feel sorry for you. But we learned from you too—how not to act and how not to conduct ourselves and be petty. We were there because the courts put the inmates there, and we were charged with their safety and security.

Was it worth it? No retirement, no insurance and no respect.

So what makes an officer a good or bad one?

The good ones helped you and showed you how to act and conduct yourself. They taught us to treat the inmates like we would want to be treated if the roles were reversed, remembering we are there not to punish, but to keep them inside, keep society safe, and minister to their needs.

The bad officers didn't give a damn about anything except themselves. They thought the rest of us were there to punish them and harass them at every opportunity and make their days miserable. Fortunately, this type usually didn't last long in the system. And some, because of their attitude, came back as inmates.

Chapter 6

THE CONVICTED

Murder. Rape. Child abuse. Child molestation. Arson, Robbery. Drug crimes. Flagrant non-support. Multiple DUIs.

These are all *felonies*. Not misdemeanors or slightly wrong. *Felonies*. The people who committed these crimes went to trial, were convicted by a jury of their peers, and are now convicted felons.

Even when they make parole, they have lost all rights, voting privileges, and the freedom to carry firearms, but some still do those things. In some cases, alcohol is forbidden. Their crimes ran the course. Most were in the headlines of the papers from the counties or cities where they lived. Some of our prisoners came to our facility from other counties or states due to high-profile cases and the need for greater security. We took one of theirs, and the other facility took one of ours . . . trades, just like in the NFL, MLB, or NBA, but not as sporting.

The prisoners had committed these crimes. They were now felons. About 85 percent of the felons at LLCC were there for sex crimes. All sex crimes are heinous, but some of the prisoners were some sick creatures. Most of the inmates claimed they were set up, were innocent, and used the common excuse, "She lied to me. She said she was eighteen." If I only had a dime for each time I heard that!

The real bad guys doing life, knowing that they will *never* get out of prison, they had some of the most interesting stories. Almost all their stories or excuses were born out of a jealous rage and the contentions, "She's mine," and, "If I can't have her no one can."

Inmate Robert's story was typical. He was young and in love and so was she until she learned of his controlling ways and hot temper. He was a big, strong muscular guy who worked in the construction business. After a long day of work and many beers later, she decided it was over for them and told him so. He became so enraged, that he was blinded by love. A love he knew was now destined to end although he desperately wanted it to continue.

He said it was a combination of the alcohol and the "green-eyed monster" that took over. He drove her out to the construction site where he was working and proceeded to do her in. He killed her by choking her to death.

Then he cut her throat.
Then he ran over her with a bulldozer.
Then he set her on fire.
Then he buried her.
Hopefully, she didn't suffer much.

He was doing life without a chance for parole, and he became a model inmate. He planted a garden when he could, worked it, and shared the rewards of his labors with other inmates. He went to church on a regular basis and volunteered at the chapel. Maybe if he had been doing those things prior to killing her . . .

He attended and graduated from anger management classes offered by the prison and became quiet and reserved. The anger classes were required by the parole board, even if there were no chance for parole. Each inmate had to see the board after a specified number of years.

He received regular visits from his family and his mail was as regular as clockwork. They didn't dwell on what he did, but once when I was working visiting, I did hear his father ask him once, after all these years in prison, "I know you regret what you did, son, but are you truly remorseful for what you did, and have you asked for forgiveness?"

Tears welled up in Robert's eyes and he said, "Yes, I did, Dad, but it's awful hard for me to admit it to myself."

Then there were the truly sick. Where these guys found it in themselves to do some of the things they did, they had to reach deep into the depths of their hellish souls.

Inmate Sandy was one of those. Just to look at him, you could tell he was never the star athlete, homecoming king, or even had many dates—if any. He attended school but never graduated, only going to the ninth grade. Not able to land or keep a steady job, he did what many do—resorted to petty crime. He got caught, went to court and received slaps on the wrist, until some judge put him in jail for short periods of time: 90 days, 120 days, 180 days with time off for good behavior. He was not very attractive, smallish in stature, and did not speak clearly. But he did land a girl. How long their relationship went on, I never found out. But he also was a control freak, prone to physical violence and abuse. Why some women stayed in these relationships, I never understood, except maybe due to low self-esteem. At any rate, one day she wised up and told him it was over. He killed her by stabbing her multiple times and leaving the body in the basement of a condemned building. He returned to visit her dead body several times over many weeks and had sex with her corpse until the stench and rot set in.

He was also doing life without parole. He was not a model inmate and was into many scams and schemes on the yard. He was caught, did his time in the "hole" (more on that later) and went back to doing what he did. But he did hold a job in the prisons, usually in his dorm doing menial things and making menial money. I never saw any visitors for him but he did receive some mail.

Another inmate who was matter of fact was Tom. When asked about his crime, he told you. He had been married for many years, had a steady job, and supported his family. His only complaint was that his "old lady" just kept nagging, nagging, and nagging on him when he got home form work. He said he had warned her many times to knock that shit off, or he would do something.

"She laughed at me once to often," he said. Tom said he punched her and knocked her out. He then shot her in the head while she lay in the bathtub. Then, to complete things, he got his chainsaw out and cut her into little pieces and buried her in the back yard in thick black trash bags. Living in the country he didn't have a lot of nosy neighbors. We asked him one day, after he related this story to us, if it had been messy.

"Matter of fact," he replied, "yes it was a little, but the chainsaw cut right through her. Bones and all." Then he added, "I bet that bitch don't f*** with me anymore."

He was still adamant that what he did was all her fault. And he was appealing his conviction. Good luck!

Not all stories are bad, and neither are all convicts.

Take the story of Fred. Family man. Wife and teenage daughter and son at home. Hardworking. He owned his own business. Then one day his world was shattered. He got a call at work to come home. He got there, and the police and his entire family were there. The police told him his fifteen-year-old daughter had been beaten and raped by her boyfriend. Mad, pissed off, fuming, thinking and planning ahead already, all Fred could do was console his daughter, son, and wife and ask questions.

"Where is he now"?

The police said they didn't know.

Fred continued to ask questions.

"Are you looking for him?"

Yes, came the response.

"When did this happen?"

"We got the report about forty-five minutes ago," the officer told him.

"Did you get him yet?"

The police told Fred they hadn't found the boyfriend yet, but they were looking.

Fred said, "Well you better find him . . . before we do."

Unfortunately, they did not. Fred and his son found him first, and beat him to death.

Justified? No! But how many of us would not want to do the same thing?

Is it sympathy or empathy?

Robbers in training. That's what Michael did. He was a body builder, tall, strong, and muscular, the leader of a gang of five to seven thugs who robbed various establishments. What they did was almost ingenious, almost. This gang made their living out of robbing various fast food establishments. They would rehearse at home, slowly and methodically going through the steps of the crime.

The day of the caper, several of them would go to the selected establishment, order some food, sit down, and eat. During the meal, upon a signal from the leader, the new guy would come, act as if he were alone, and rob the place. After he was gone and the police showed up, the clues, descriptions, the way he was dressed, mannerisms, everything was different from each eye witnesses. I wondered why. They were all in on it. After a while, the police wised up because the places getting robbed almost always had some of this gang as witnesses. The best laid plans of mice and men . . .

Drugs. The downfall of a lot of people . . . good and bad. It was a poison that ate you up, and had you chasing that high you first felt. But it never came again. The addict had to use more drugs to get that same high. The next time it was more drugs to get *that* high. The vicious circle was never complete.

He *had been* a professional athlete. He *had been* in a Super Bowl. He *was* a drug user. He *was* a drug transporter. He got caught up in the drug scene, got sentenced to several years. He did his time and made parole in a December just before New Year's Day. He was back inside within ninety days. Got caught . . . again. He did several more years, finished his time (killed his bit, as the inmates say), and went home. Next we heard about him was that he died from an overdose of heroin. A life wasted. Great talent wasted. All because of chasing a high that was never there.

Another inmate had been a GI, on leave and heading to his port in New Jersey to go overseas to Germany. He had already completed a tour in Viet Nam so he was a combat vet. He knew how to be stealthy, quiet, and sneaky. And how to kill silently. He had stopped over in Kentucky and spent several days at a preacher's house there, arranged through a friend. But the GI was not friendly around the preacher's daughter. He did some dastardly things to her and killed her, then hid the body in a closet in the spare bedroom he had been using. He left and made it all the way to New Jersey before the body was found. After a very short investigation and a confession, he was brought back to Kentucky, tried, convicted, and sentenced to life without parole.

There are hundreds of stories yet to be told. Maybe there will be another book.

Chapter 7

WHO DO YOU TRUST?

Is trusting in someone equal to that person "having your back?"

In every job, you have to know who's got your back. In all walks of life, it is necessary to know that, no matter what you do, someone will be watching out for you. Sometimes, it's that someone is watching you; there are the ones who just cannot wait for you to make a mistake and then they run, run, run as fast as they can to turn you in. I guess they think they are making themselves look better.

Sure, mistakes were made, but hopefully we all learned from them. I know I certainly did. But the best colleagues were those you could trust and rely on without hesitation, a person or partner who knew your next move instinctively and could anticipate things before they happened. Call it a sixth sense or a gut feeling, but it was usually right. After all, your life was in those hands, literally. I had several of those partners over the years.

One of them, Sue, was always a straight shooter. She knew her job, took no crap from any convict, and yet showed a compassionate side when needed. We clicked as a team, and it sometimes paid off when one of us had a hunch . . . that feeling you got in the pit of your stomach when you knew something just wasn't right . . . and she had it on more than one occasion. It paid off when she found stashes of drugs and several tattoo guns with all the equipment and ink. The needles were made from ink pens, motors made from cassette recorders, ink made and mixed from the print shop. She was always good to work with, and I trusted her.

Then there was the dude. We worked together for about one and a half years on two different shifts, second and first. He was a lanky guy who always knew what was going on, and was always suspicious of the inmates and staff . . . more times than not, more suspicious of the staff, as he was a bit paranoid. But he had a way to get information. Some staff and some inmates thought he was really a rube, but he knew what was happening and played it to his advantage. He had even done a stint in the army and was a military policeman, so he had to have his ducks in a row.

He had a few informants who let him know when something big was about to happen or where something was hidden. More than once he found shanks (prison knives) or other contraband. He always was outgoing, knew his job, and did it well. He paid attention to details, and this gave him an edge over most. If it didn't look like a duck . . .

One of the worst officers I knew was a guy who was demoted from sergeant. To say he was in a bad mood would be putting it mildly. And everywhere he went, he thought he still was a sergeant and in charge . . . didn't like to listen to others or take orders because he knew it all.

Oh, and he had connections in Frankfort . . . especially when he got his sergeant stripes back. Then he was really hard to work around.

His run-in with me was my fault but there were different ways to handle situations. One could talk to the person or just go hang the officer out to dry. The day this happened, we were both working in Special Management Unit, SMU, the hole. It was an extremely busy day. We had a full house, forty inmates. We still had to do our daily duties, change linens, feed, do pill call, get them outside for recreation, and see to medical visits, among others. We were having one of *those* days. We were in the process of releasing two inmates back to the yard, and locking up two others. The other floor officer needed a ring of keys because it had the storage room keys on it. I committed *the* number one officer crime in prison. I gave a set of keys to an inmate and watched him take them to an officer less then twenty-five feet away. I watched him the whole time.

This key ring had only the following keys on it: the bathroom; the storage room with linens, blankets, and pillow cases in it, located outside, upstairs, through two locked, electronically controlled doors, that I was in control of; and storage lockers in the janitor area. That's all. No more. But this guy saw fit to raise hell with me. Yes, I was wrong.

Then he went and wrote a letter telling what I had done to the deputy warden of security. Worse, he tried to pass it off as though it had been written by the inmate to whom I gave the keys. The problem here was that the inmate had no access to the mailbox where the letter was dropped. But the shit hit the fan.

I had DWs, captains, and IA in SMU asking me if I had really given my keys to an inmate. I said yes, and gave my explanation why and explained what keys were on that key ring. I had to put on paper an occurrence report about what I had done. Several days later I got my formal letter of reprimand.

What I did was wrong. There is no gray area. But what he did went overboard.

Those keys posed no security risk and could not open any doors that went to any sensitive areas. Yeah, I learned a lot about him that day. But he did this to many other officers, trying to make himself seem bigger and better.

After he got the shit beat out of him by some inmates, he quit, resigned. I guess he just couldn't handle the *real* bad guys.

I think that happened because he had no one's back, not even his own, in the long run.

But looking back, I see that, if you didn't trust your partner, they didn't trust you, and that could lead to him or her looking the other way for just a second at the wrong time, or responding, but just not as fast as necessary. And that could have an effect on your safety, your life.

Trust was a two-way street.

Chapter 8

PROGRAMS AVAILABLE TO INMATES

It took more than a bunch of officers, sergeants, lieutenants, and captains to make a prison run. The program staff were the ones who ran the dorms, the print shop, gymnasium, kitchen, chapel, gym, medical, and all other programs offered to inmates. They were nonuniformed staff. Some started as officers and worked their way up the ladder, so they knew what the officers were doing each and every day. All program locations were staffed by uniformed and nonuniformed staff. The nonuniformed personnel were there to administer the programs, instruct, and oversee the inmates' progress in that particular class or area. The uniformed staff provided security and monitored tool usage and tool inventory. They were also responsible to frisk-search all inmates as they left the area where they worked. This was to insure no tools or materials were carried out of the areas back to the dorms. Any and all items could be considered weapons or be made into them.

The nonuniformed staff provided jobs for the inmates, and some jobs paid a decent wage, considering they were in prison. Wages ran from eighty-five cents per day to about $1.85 per hour plus overtime in certain jobs. Jobs in the prison ran from unit janitors to press operators in the print shop, kitchen workers who did the cooking, and stocking and unloaded the food trucks, all under the supervision of staff.

All knives are chained to the tables, with just enough length to reach the tabletop for work, so they didn't have to be under constant supervision at several work stations.

To get the better jobs, inmates had to meet certain criteria: clear conduct for at least six months and a minimum of five years to your serve-out date or parole. The prison didn't like turn over in "employees" either. It cost to train them, and the longer they stayed, the more productive they became. And they enjoyed the money they made.

Some of the things they printed were state posters, handicap parking tags, envelopes, food stamps (before they had the debit card system), and paper temporary license plate tags for new cars. The print shop program made money for the state as well, because all state programs that needed anything printed had to go through the bidding process, and the prison had a chance to bid also.

The data processing program was another moneymaker for the state.

The state bid on jobs to input information into various systems. Inmates processed coupons from various sources, telemarketing info, and credit card purchases. *No* private information was available to the inmates. These inmates had to pass a typing test. They had a lot of work to do and often worked overtime. Yes, there was overtime in prison and they earned it after meeting their regular number of weekly hours. They enjoyed the work and made a decent wage. It helped pass the time for them. And the more money they made inside, the less they had to ask for from their families.

One of the better programs for the inmates was "Shakespeare Behind Bars." It was a program where the inmates played the major Shakespearean roles. They did the set design, made props and backdrops, and learned their lines. There were about twelve inmates who did this on a regular basis (now up to about thirty). They were taught by a group of professionals from outside the prison who came in, helped tutor, and encouraged the inmates as well as made sure the productions came off without a hitch. The plays when ready were performed for the prison staff and families who wanted to see them. All plays were conducted in the inmates' visiting room. Again, clear conduct was a prerequisite for this privilege.

Another program was SOTP, or Sex Offender Treatment Program. This was usually mandated for the inmates either by the courts or parole board, as a condition when appearing before the parole board, after they had met their minimum sentence requirements.

Anger management was another court-mandated program. It was supposed to teach the inmates how to control their anger so they could continue what they were doing under the most stressful situations in real life outside of prison. Sometimes it worked and sometimes it didn't. Those who just couldn't take direction or follow instructions or orders always failed the course. Some were given more than one chance to go through it and several wanted to do it more than once just so they could be sure of themselves when they got out.

There were organized sports, except football. The basketball and softball teams played each other by dorms, and occasionally teams from outside the prison came in and played the inmates. These were usually church groups, and after the games they talked to the inmates and tried to help them lead a better life directed to God.

Some of the other programs were auto mechanics, wood shop, masonry, plumbing, and electrical. These were taught from both the basic to advanced levels to give inmates skills they could use once they got out.

Those inmates who didn't qualify for the better jobs got jobs in their dorms, or outside jobs such as grass cutters, dorm janitors, maintenance, or sidewalk sweepers. The only benefit the sweepers had was that they picked up the discarded cigarette butts and recycled them by taking the tobacco out and keeping it, then buying rolling papers to make fresh cigarettes—a great way to save money on tobacco, but who knew what diseases they were also picking up?

Different prisons had different programs that benefitted that particular prison or the state in general. Some of the other prisons and what they did were:

- KSR made the Kentucky license plates, state soap, and did some metal work such as wall lockers and desks.

- KSP made the uniforms used in the prison system.
- KCIW had Paws for Purpose, where the inmates trained dogs to become service dogs.
- BCC made plastic stackable chairs, folding tables, and refurbished computers.
- RCC had a program to allow an inmate to become a horticulture technician.

All the state prisons had programs, and they all had education programs whereby inmates were afforded the opportunity to finish high school and to start and complete college degrees. They also had AA/NA programs, so once in the system they are not just locked away and forgotten about. Hopefully, they can learn to overcome their addictions.

Eventually, after much debate, the prison system allowed the inmates in the honor dorms to buy and have mailed in video games and consoles as long as they came from approved DOC vendors. No games could be rated X or show any sex, and all were subject to inspection upon arrival in the mail.

All this takes place while the prisoners serve their time. They learn a trade to keep them from returning to prison. Some chose to rehabilitate themselves, while others didn't.

There was one inmate who took legal courses in prison and worked as a legal aide to other inmates. He was good. When his parole appearance came, he was granted parole and got out. He then got a job in a law firm doing research and looking up case law, and helping those who were less fortunate. He was truly rehabilitated and gave back to society.

The goal of the prison system is not just to punish the inmates for their crimes and rehabilitate the inmates, but to prevent recidivism, and make them proud, productive members of society. But they had to apply themselves and want to change. Going back to same old neighborhood, running with same old gang of friends (who didn't bother to visit while you were incarcerated) didn't help. Inmates had to break their old habits and old lifestyles if the change was going to stick on the outside.

Various volunteer groups came and visited the inmates. All offered encouragement and some had the promise of helping them to find jobs, get an apartment, learn to use ATMs or cell phones, get a driver's license back, just the everyday things we take for granted. Shopping, keeping a checkbook. Things they haven't seen or done in years to help them get back into the mainstream of society.

Information on all state prisons as well as the programs available to inmates can be found online. (www.corrections.ky.gov).

Chapter 9

STAFF ASSISTANCE

Most of the staff cared about what they did. Some didn't give a shit, and the other staff and inmates knew who they were. Most officers who cared tried to stay away from those who didn't because they were going to be trouble. Oh, they did their jobs, but just barely and not a bit more. Some couldn't wait to go home. Some were a bit too intimate—"friendly," if you know what I mean—but they always got caught. It went back to Joe told Bob who told Mike who told Sam, and soon . . . you get the picture. There were *no* secrets in prison.

Some program staff were a positive influence on some of the inmates. They made inmates believe in themselves and encouraged them to seek out programs that would help them help themselves. Staff showed a positive attitude and image, and some inmates saw that and tried even harder. Maybe those convicts just wanted to show *somebody* that they could do *something* good. The program staff member was the go-to person for the inmate. If the inmate wanted or needed anything, he had to go through his CTO. If the inmate wanted a job recommendation, special visit, or change to his visiting list, he had to see his CTO.

And then there were the bad apples.

We had one CTO who liked the bottle . . . a lot. The inmates called him "Mr. Hungover," because he usually was. Some days he came to work smelling like a honky-tonk tavern on a Sunday morning. Although the front desk officer noticed the smell on several occasions, if he was refused entry, he went home and called in sick. If the paperwork wasn't done correctly, and if a breathalyzer was not given properly, things went his way, but at least he was now given notice and the officials could keep an eye on him. Or he could tell his supervisor that he had a problem and go to treatment and get off because he had a "problem," but he would still be watched. Eventually his old habits returned, the same process happened again, and eventually he was terminated. But it was a l-o-o-o-ng process.

There was another CTO who liked to eat the prison food. The Tater, a name given to him by the inmates and not used around the staff much, was a bachelor and if it couldn't be cooked in a microwave, it didn't get cooked by him. While attending college, he lived at home, and while his mother did all his cooking, he never learned to cook for himself, so he liked to eat as many meals as he could at the prison. I don't know what he did on weekends . . . maybe went home, or maybe ate a lot of fast food. However, he devised a plan. He made a deal with some janitors where he worked to save him any extra food trays. He in turn brought sacks of potatoes. He would trade taters for food trays. After all, potatoes were cheap, inmates liked them, and they were expensive for the inmates. The inmates would set aside any extra trays and when he came to work, the swap was made. Only it was illegal and against the code of ethics. This went on for awhile, but as mentioned before, there were no secrets in prison. He was caught, given a letter of reprimand, and he too was eventually fired, because he couldn't listen. Guess he was a fried tater!!

Mr. Tater was not a real "people person." He had no personality and kept to himself. A real dud spud! We had exchanged words on several occasions. The last time was before he left. At the height of the confrontation, I told him that he had *zero,* I mean *zero* personality skills. The supervisor on site ordered me to leave Tater's office because he knew that I was going to unload and let him have it. I guess it was for the best because I was pissed and had had enough of his bullshit! But he just continued his trading ways until it was discovered that no matter how many times we reported it, he was still making these trades, and then he was terminated. He finally got mashed! His incompetence caused other staff to have to do or redo his job, correct his errors, and help the inmates he was supposed to have helped.

The kitchen staff (nonuniformed) used to take turns bringing in food on Sunday mornings for their staff. IA had been tipped off to one who was bringing in drugs, mostly marijuana, instead of food. IA had been watching "Mary Jane" for some time. One Sunday when it was her turn, she brought in a case of hamburgers that the inmates craved. She was let in past the front desk check-in officer and made it through the first set of the electronic controlled doors.

There she was greeted by IA and the KSP. They checked the case, and *lo and behold,* the secret spice on the burgers was marijuana in little plastic bags. She was escorted to TAD, put in an orange jumpsuit, handcuffed, and escorted out. As the old song goes, "another one bites the dust."

Now the kitchen was one staff short for serving the breakfast meal and the rest of the staff had to pick up her slack. I wondered how she explained that to her husband and two kids. Long-range repercussions.

Another kitchen staff was having an affair with an inmate kitchen worker. Some times inmates were allowed to stay at their place of work during counts. They were then placed on an out-count sheet (meaning they were counted in their workplace instead of their dorm) and counted in place. During counts there was no movement of inmates and all staff were in dorms helping to count inmates and *all* doors were locked. That left the staff and inmate alone for at least twenty to thirty minutes. Ah, the stolen moments of love. Only this couple could not leave it at work.

Above all phones there were signs that said *"ALL PHONE CALLS ARE SUBJECT TO BE MONITORED."* One never knew who was listening. All calls were recorded, staff and inmate, just in case they need to be replayed later for any reason.

When confronted about their affair, they both denied it but they were busted. IA played the tapes back, with the kitchen staff's husband present. He also worked in the prison. Talk about red faced!! Whoop, there it was! She was fired and he retired shortly thereafter.

Don't get me wrong. There were *many* good staff workers in prison, and many good stories about them, the good jobs they did, and the caring they showed.

The staff also had the unenviable job of telling an inmate the tragic news when a loved one had been in an accident or died. Sometimes the inmate knew especially if someone was sick. The CTOs arranged for bedside hospital visits or trips to funerals. But they were always limited to one hour and always under the watchful eyes of at least two officers.

But cons being cons, the inmates often tried to use the visits to score drugs or other contraband, i.e., tobacco, weapons, or cell phones, among others. The common excuse was, "I have to use the bathroom." They were never allowed to be alone for that reason. At some funerals families were not allowed to touch or hug or kiss. Things could be easily passed. Sometimes on these visits, family arguments broke out. The anger was usually directed at the inmate, with other family members saying things like, "Look what you did to our mother/ father. They were fine till you went to prison and then all they did was worry about your sorry ass." And, "Every time you call, all you do is ask for money, and you know she didn't have it."

I've seen the biggest, baddest, hardest inmate break down and cry at the loss of a loved one, trying to cram years of regret and sorrow into one hour. Sometimes the tragic experience changed them, and we noticed after they returned to the confines of the prison. And for some, it just wore off and then it was life as usual.

Chapter 10

INMATE LIVING AREAS

There were five different living dorms, classified 7A, 7B, 7C, 7D, and 7E and segregation. Each was unique and served a different purpose.

Outside each dorm was a fenced-in area with gates that were locked at various times. This allowed the inmates to be released when it time for smoke break, which was generally once an hour (until prisons go tobacco-free), until lights out at eleven p.m. The lock-up times depended on the rank or status of that dorm. As an example, 7A being a new convicts' dorm, was afforded less mobility and freedom and access to the yard. E, being more "dependable" and sometimes working late, had more privileges; therefore, their gates stayed open longer.

The fenced area was about four hundred square feet. These fenced areas were called "bull pens." They were under cover and open on all sides and usually contained six picnic tables where the inmates could sit and relax, scheme their deals, plan any dastardly deeds, play dominoes or cards, or just shoot the shit. These areas also were used by some inmates to grow small gardens and flowerbeds. The dorms liked to compete amongst themselves to see who could grow the better flowers, bigger melons, etc. Some even grew tomato plants and watermelons and cantaloupes, among other fruits and veggies.

7A

This dorm was mainly used for new arrivals. They were assigned there so they could be classified as to weaknesses and strengths and to see if they had any conflicts on the yard with codefendants. These conflicts ranged from someone whom they may have committed a crime with or against their families, to someone they may have testified against in court or who testified against them. Remember the old adage, "no honor amongst thieves."

Inmates were assessed so that a variety of social and academic capabilities or conditions could be determined for placement in programs the inmates needed, wanted, or were court-ordered to take. They were screened to see if they qualified for any jobs, such as prison industries, print shop, kitchen, maintenance assistants, data, library, and others. Also by being in this dorm, they were more controlled on the yard as they learned the rules and regulations, the coming and goings, the different time schedules for various programs, and for eating. Even eating happened on a rotating basis because of the vast number of people to be fed. All dorms posted the menu on the bulletin boards, and when the food was "good," they all tried to line up early.

Others who stayed in this dorm were those who couldn't find a job or didn't want a job. There were a bunch of those. If they couldn't find a job, they were given menial tasks to do in the dorm but nobody just lay around all day doing nothing, and everyone had to make their bed by eight a.m. After that they could lay on it, but not under the covers. None of the inmates liked this dorm because of the controls placed on them.

7B and C

These two dorms were almost identical. After an inmate's orientation time was up in 7A and he became acclimated to the way the prison worked, he moved into one of these dorms. Acclimation included more than just learning the basic rules of the prison. It was also who did what on the yard, establishing contacts on the yard and forming alliances, and planning their "extracurricular" activities, like gambling, running book, working for someone else doing the same things, getting in on the drug trade, or doing the right thing by looking for or getting a job or going to school. After all, it was hard to come in a "fish" and take over anything. They got their jobs, either on the yard or in the dorm. They were also offered the opportunity to play a variety of sports, depending on the season: softball, basketball, football (no tackle). They also spent a lot of time in the gym. They played foosball, ping pong, weight lifting, exercise bikes, pool, handball, and paddle ball. The only constant was weightlifting. *Many* did this and they bulked up . . . a lot. Besides, what else did they have to do, all day, every day, day in, day out for years on end during their nonworking hours? They played eight ball, bumper pool, any kind of pool games, cards, betting sports (for cigarettes), but they tried not to get caught. If they didn't pay up at the end of the night, there was interest added. Then it was noted somewhere and trouble could begin.

If your debt wasn't paid it was sold to a "collector" and the debt increased until paid. Debts in prison never go away. There were even instances when a person got out on parole, then came back on a new charge and found the debt was still there. Then it was collected.

From these two dorms, inmates could apply to moves to other dorms depending on status or job assignment.

7D

This was considered one of the honor dorms. It housed inmates who had been in for a long time. They were generally quieter; they just wanted to do their time, do their jobs, and be left alone.

Some of the maintenance workers, such as the plumbers and electricians who were on call all day and night, because of their expertise, were housed in 7D. They were also afforded access to restricted areas as long as they were escorted by an officer or a maintenance staff. In addition to being escorted, they were monitored by the outside perimeter patrol officer in a car, and by the nearest guard tower. The officers in the towers had weapons available to them.

Inmates in this dorm also earned additional privileges by their good behavior. Some of these were later nights (lights out), more freedom of movement in the dorm, more items kept in their rooms (food, game consoles), access to more games in the wings, (card games and board games), and microwave ovens, although eventually all dorms had those. They also received visits during the week and their visitors were allowed to bring in food from outside fast food restaurants. Another perk was an extra visit on Friday night. These visits were only two extra hours, but they were a welcome addition to other visits on the weekends and holidays.

7E

This was also an honor dorm. It had the same privileges as 7D, but this dorm also had inmates who were required to attend various classes. If these classes were not completed, or if they failed to attend or were kicked out or removed for any reason, they were immediately sent to another dorm and they had to reapply to get accepted back into the class. This removal class was noted in their records jacket and available for review by the parole board when the inmate went for his parole hearing. Some of the classes were SOTP (Sex Offender Treatment Program), anger management, and drug awareness, AA/NA (Alcohol Anonymous/Narcotics Anonymous). Not completing the course (s) you were required to attend could be grounds for not making parole.

There was a saying on the yard that if you wanted drugs, go to 7E. Somehow they seemed to filter in there. Most contraband is brought in by staff and visitors, although some made it in through the mail, even though all mail was opened and checked.

These inmates also had a small exercise yard in their dorm yard area. It was equipped with weight-lifting apparatus, a small walking track, and pull up bars.

While all the dorms housed inmates, some good, some bad, and the honor dorms housed "honor" inmates, all inmates were sneaky and capable of deceit. They had mastered the art of telling tales, stories, lies and half truths, incomplete stories, and deflecting blame from themselves to others. In prison, the best way to get your ass kicked or worse was to be labeled a rat or snitch or be thought of as one. Once that tag was attached to you it stuck with you until . . .

The easiest way to survive was to keep in mind, "I didn't see or hear anything," and to keep one's mouth shut!

Remember the three monkeys? See nothing, hear nothing, and say nothing.

A lot of folks forgot this and have paid the price. A favorite warning was, "Remember that snitches get stitches."

A "stinger" in prison is a piece of metal that's plugged into an electrical outlet. It's about six inches long and is meant to heat water in a cup. Once plugged in, it gets hot *fast* and is sometimes used to brand inmates as a reminder: "Shut your damn mouth!"

If a person was suspected of being a snitch, he was usually visited at a time when there was little officer presence in the dorm. At feeding times, during counts when the officers are in one wing and attention is focused there, the snitch is usually dragged into a room and the "hit squad," who get paid in stamps or cigarettes, then beats the shit out of the snitch either with fists, or a bar of soap, or a lock, or rocks in a sock. It makes a *very* brutal weapon. The attack usually wasn't discovered until the count officer finds a bloody person, either conscious or unconscious, while clearing the floor for count. And if the attacks were bad enough, split heads were often found, emergencies called, and count delayed. That lets everyone know something happened. To those who ordered the hit, it meant mission accomplished.

The room assignments were usually made by the UA (Unit Administrator) assigned to each dorm. The UA was the senior nonofficer staff assigned to a dorm. The CTOs or case workers and officers worked for him or her.

Roomies were usually paired according to race and age closeness if possible. Similar interests, same work assignments. Sometimes they got along; sometimes they didn't. Inmates could ask to be moved into cells with a certain person, as they usually got along together, worked together, and sometimes went to school together back home. Some were even paired where one person did the housework and the other did the outside work, and together they supported each other. Sometimes one was the protector, in exchange for sexual favors. Yes, it was a prison and it does happen! It went on . . . a lot. As officers, it was hard (pardon the pun) to be everywhere, and see what was going on. But when they did get caught, they went straight to the hole . . . another pun intended!

All dorms had between 180 and 220 inmates, twenty-four to twenty-eight per floor. There were two floors per wing, four wings per dorm, each wing floor with one shower, three toilets, and two urinals. There were no windows or doors to open, thus enclosing all that urine smell, body odor, foot stink, inmates farting and burping in a small area. Some didn't shower every day. Some waited every two or three days. That smell smacked you straight in the face every time you entered a dorm. It was a smell you never forgot. You could only hope it washed off when you got home.

There were two inmates per cell and the overflow in dorms 7 A, B, C stayed in the open common areas on day beds. No cells . . . yet. Too overcrowded.

There are usually only two officers per dorm, one on the floor to meet call ins or perform other duties and requirements, and one in the control center. So figuring that one officer is not in contact with any inmates, that's one, *one* officer for all those inmates on the floor. In four wings. That's a lot of watching to do. Approximately 180 to 1 odds. Would you bet on anything with those odds? The officers did, every day—with their lives. Considering that the floor officer had to issue daily supplies to the inmate janitors, conduct security checks, do patrols, monitor who came and went, conduct counts, respond when and where needed, search inmates and cells, find the contraband if they could. The inmates have twenty-fours a day, every day to hide it. You had seven and a half hours to find it, plus do all the other things mentioned above. Oh, and don't forget to take your thirty-minute lunch break.

The control center officer primarily watches the floor officer as he does his job, plus he has all the paperwork to do, answer the phones, coordinate the inmate moves between dorms, assist the floor officer in count, locate inmates to send to medical, TAD, job workplaces, or wherever else they are needed/wanted.

The dorms after dark

There are a lot of stories of the dorms *after* dark. This is when the most nasty, dirty events happen. This is because it's dark, the lights are turned low, and the doors make a lot of noise when they are opened or closed, thus giving ample warning to those inside. It's metal on metal and slamming shut when they close. When they open and close, it signals everyone someone is coming in and it's usually the staff doing count or making patrols. Some inmates time these patrols so they can "get busy." Getting busy usually means having sex.

Yes, it does happen in prison, both willingly and non-willingly. Debts are paid, favors paid, and collected. For whatever reason, it happens. If and when the floor officer making patrols finds such things going on, the first reaction is disgust. Then the inmates are both sent to the hole. After their time in seg, they are usually sent to different dorms to keep them separated. Sometimes it works; sometimes it doesn't.

The officers who work the night shift are aware of what happens and when and with whom, so they happen to catch more. And there is usually a story that goes with each one. But we've seen it all and heard it all. The best one was two inmates, one sitting on the other's lap, both naked and one getting rubbed with baby oil on his back saying, "He's just rubbing me with oil." But neither one wanted to stand up. Things that make you say hmm . . . And, yes, both went to the hole.

Almost all inmates knew who was involved and let it be. The number one rule in prison among inmates is, if it's not your business, keep your nose out of it. And always remember, you didn't see anything and you don't know anything. Always *mind your own business.*

A few reminders were usually written and posted someplace in the dorm wings:

If it's not yours—don't touch it.

If it's not broke—don't screw with it.

If it's yours—lock it up.

If it doesn't concern you—move on.

Remember—snitches get stitches.

Chapter 11

THE YARD—IS IT AN ESCAPE OR REMINDER?

The yard is the huge open area of the prison. It consists of approximately six to eight acres. This includes the recreation areas and ball fields, volleyball court, outdoor weightlifting area, and handball courts plus the walking and running tracks. The yard is where inmates spend most of their time walking, talking, and keeping up on their friends. They scheme their deeds and plans, their goings on, and are only monitored by sight and not sound, so they are able to talk freely. The ones with no jobs just walk all day and shoot the breeze. It's their version of the mall, the big box stores, and the block back home. It's mostly grass with a sidewalk that goes around and through it. The grass is off limits, unless you have business there. There are areas designated for flowers and gardens that are tended to by inmates. They grow an array of flowers, and some beds were designated for fruits, and veggies, just like in the dorm bull pens.

Not all inmates are given this privilege. It has to be earned and then approved by the CTO and UA, with the warden giving final approval. The inmates who are approved are given a small piece of ground, usually ten by ten, to use.

All tools are checked out from maintenance and used under the supervision of an officer. This means they cannot tend their spots every day, as the officers have other duties to perform. The inmates plant, weed, and water their gardens. After the growing season they enjoy the fruits of their labors and usually share with their friends in the dorms, or sell the items or trade for what they need or want. After all, fresh melons and watermelons are not common in prison.

There are other types of business going on as well. Neither rain, nor snow, nor heat of day shall keep these inmates from their appointed rounds. There are gangs in prison and this is where they do their business. There were Bloods, Crips, blacks, whites, Hispanics, and all had their gangs or cliques. Plans were made for the ass-kickings, collection of debts, and retribution for those who didn't pay up. The leaders of the different areas, i.e., drugs, betting, collections, loan sharking, etc., pass out the instructions to be carried out.

Past-due accounts are resold to others. For the weak ones, the yard was a matter of delaying the inevitable. Debts had to be paid. If you incurred a debt, you suffered the consequences of the beatings but you still owed the debt. The debts never went away until paid-in full. The wheeler-dealers in the prison conduct a lot of business here. They walk, talk, pass on information, and pass notes, betting slips, and other contraband here. There are about 1,200 inmates at LLCC, and on a good day, 60 total officers. Not good odds, and there a lot of folks to watch considering not all staff and inmates were on the yard at any given time. All dorms have to be staffed, program areas staffed, all posts manned, which leaves only a few to monitor the yard and only a few in the towers to watch the whole yard area. (Due to security matters no more can be revealed about these towers.) At any one time, there are about three hundred inmates walking the yard in all directions, doing various things, going to different areas, some legit, some not. So the officers watch, looking for something that just doesn't seem right, and they just do they best they can. They usually spend more time watching those who are known to be leaders in the illegal activities.

It's cat and mouse everyday, with us watching them watching us watching them.

While all state prisons are similar in nature, they all have their own specific rules governing movement, housing, and job assignments, etc., and if some inmates liked a more structured daily routine, they asked to be transferred to a particular prison. Some did so because they were trying to stay with known friends or acquaintances, or maybe someone they had gone to school with, or they were following their debts. Inmates think and do funny things.

Chapter 12

ILLEGAL ACTIVITIES

There were many items and types of contraband within the walls of the prison. The inmates made them, hid them, and improved the ones they had, all the while trying to stay ahead of the staff. After all, they had 24 hours a day, 7 days a week, 365 days a year to plot and plan, while the officers had seven and a half hours a day to find them and still do all their other tasks. Things that make you say hmm. Sometimes the officers win, sometimes the inmates win. Both sides know this and it was a constant "game" we played. But we had an edge; we looked every day and we asked questions of the right inmates, and we had informants to help us.

It took a long time to cultivate an informant, but once you got a good one, you protected him. You didn't let him get away with any crimes, but on minor issues, you sometime looked the other way and had an officer remind him he was also being watched. But one thing you learned after you had a good informant—you *never* gave up his name. Everyone knew that, but IA usually figured out who your snitch was. It had to be this way to protect the inmate from retaliation from other inmates on the yard, so you could keep on getting information.

Drugs
There were both the legal and illegal kinds. The legal ones were given to inmates at pill call times for various medical problems.

These drugs were bought, sold, and traded on the yard, even after they were dispensed, taken, and had been in someone's mouth. The pills were dispensed at the pill call window and taken in front of an officer. Then the inmates had to show their hands, open their mouths, and lift their tongues to show that they were not hiding anything. But a small pill in a big mouth—it's an easy thing to do. They can and they did. As they walked away, they would remove the stashed pill, pocket it, and go on to sell it, trade it, or whatever they had in mind. Sometimes they just kept the pills for themselves, for later, in case they ever wanted to zonk out, get high, or attempt a suicide try. If caught, they went straight to SMU. Medical personnel then reevaluated the patient to determine if he still needed the drug, because, after all, if he hadn't been taking it, he might not need it. If the doctors decided he did need it, perhaps the pill could be crushed or administered in a liquid form.

The inmates never seemed to care that it was dangerous to take someone else's medication, especially after it had been in that someone's mouth.

Shanks and shivs

These were the weapon of choice on the yard. They were relatively easy to make from whatever inmates could find, steal, or fashion. Shanks, shivs, or homemade knives were made from various items. The wire that holds the fence to the fencepost might not be removed in one try, but they'll work at it for a long time to get it and it's hard to notice when one is missing, even with fence checks every day. Once they obtain it, they sharpen it by rubbing it on the sidewalks, and then they make a handle for it by wrapping one end in tape or string unraveled from a bed sheet or a pair of pants and maybe taping a stick to the end. Their ideas were endless. A toothbrush could be scraped on the floor or a sidewalk somewhere until there was a nice point on it, or they melted razor blades into the handle end of a toothbrush, and you had one hell of a knife. It sliced nastily, and the razor blade was definitely *not* a clean new one.

Shanks were pieces of metal taken (smuggled) from the different shop areas. Even when the best security measures were in place, things got smuggled out from the maintenance shop, automotive shop, and from the wood shop. Anywhere and anything they could use to fashion a weapon was used . . . Some of the more ingenious ones came from the sides of leg braces, wheelchair parts, food carts, and ice machines. The possibilities were endless. That's why the officers always had to be vigilant, keeping their eyes open and checking everything every day! Attention to detail mattered.

Once the inmates had made the weapons, they had to find hiding places for them—hiding places that were close, readily accessible, and couldn't be traced back to them if the weapon was discovered.

One potential hiding place was the ceiling tiles in the showers, which provided access to the pipes. Others included the inside of hollow shower curtain rods; under floor mats that were seldom moved or used; or buried just below the surface of the ground and marked for easy and quick retrieval and use if needed. If found, the weapon was usually in a common area, with no fingerprints, and was "not mine" no matter who we asked.

Can lids

Lids from cans of tuna, soup, mack jack (mackerel fish), and other canned goods sold at the inmate commissary were folded in half and used as knives. The edges were jagged and nasty. These were also used to slice tomatoes, potatoes, onions, and other veggies that went into the soups, stews, and noodles.

When someone got cut with a can lid, it left a nasty jagged slice that was hard to stitch up. Once used, the makeshift knives were usually just thrown away or dropped in place. It was easy to obtain another one, and hard to trace the used one.

Needles

These were harder to get a hold of. The only people who had access to needles were medical staff, and the needles were monitored closely. Even the diabetics had to go to medical to get their insulin shots. Nobody was allowed to carry any needles. Even the officers had to keep them in the captain's office. Vaccinations and all regular immunizations had to be monitored, but somehow some needles just disappeared. The inmates were fast and sneaky. If the nurse turned her head for a second and the officer was not vigilant, POOF! Gone . . . like magic.

When inmates went out on medical trips to the hospital, dentist, or emergency room, they had to be watched even more than usual, because the officer and inmate were now both in unfamiliar surroundings, and sometimes the staff at the hospitals or doctors office just didn't understand the risk involved. These inexperienced medical personnel would sometimes leave things out and unsecured in plain sight.

When a needle was obtained by an inmate, it was used, reused, and reused over and again without a second thought. Oh, it was "cleaned" with soap and water or in boiled water from the microwave, bleach sometimes when they could get some, but that was the extent of the "sterilization" process.

And the inmates would always say they didn't have anything to worry about. Yeah, right!

Tattoo guns

Tattooing in prison was a *big* business and a *big* problem. Tattoo guns were made from the motors of Walkman cassette players and other small electronic devices, and powered by batteries. Convicts adapted the workings into an ink pen and used the ink to make tattoos. Occasionally, some colored ink was smuggled out of the print shop and then sold or traded to the tattoo artists for other goods. Some of these tattoo artists were quite good, but even so, most prison tattoos were black or dark blue ink and lacked the quality of a professional tattoo shop.

When a wing door opened, it was a signal for someone to check and see who was coming or going, or to quit until it was safe to restart. A lookout was usually posted to help look out for five-o or the po-po, as they called us. (Remember *Hawaii Five-O*)? The tools were easily dismantled and easily hidden. Most "tats" took place in the dorms, in the quiet of a room, when there was usually only one officer around, or late at night when the officers were busy doing other chores.

Some of the tattoo "artists" were not that at all. Oh, they did tats, but they were not street quality. These were the ones that left nasty cuts, and the tattoo usually ended up getting infected. One trip to medical and it was discovered, triggering another investigation into illegal activities.

As with the needles mentioned above, the tattoo guns were "sterilized," but the tattoo artists did try harder to keep their tattoo guns clean.

The inmates had various ways to carry out their works, and if the officer didn't know where to look, he looked everywhere but the right place. By the time the officer figured it out, it was generally too late. I and several other officers found several tattoo guns wrapped in plastic or rags and hidden behind toilets or urinals. There were two urinals and three stools for each floor in the dorm, shared by forty-four inmates. How clean could they have been? Makes you wonder if this is one of the ways hepatitis was spread.

Alcohol

Hooch. Booze. Stink water. Home brew. Whatever other names people had, it was all the same. It was illegal, and it was made in prison. The state gave the inmates everything they needed to make it. We fed them three times a day and gave them all the fixin's. And all these items can be purchased in the inmate canteen.

Yeast. We gave it to them in bread, rolls, and baked goods.

Sugar. We gave them sugar in packets for coffee, tea, cereal, and oatmeal.

Fruit. We gave them apples, bananas, oranges, peaches, etc.

Breakfast, lunch, dinner.

Snack cakes were a big seller in prison, both as a snack and for making hooch. Mix it in the right proportions, add a little juice or water, put it in a dark warm place, and . . . wait. The longer it sat, the stronger it got both in taste, alcohol content, and *smell*.

Prison hooch had its own peculiar smell that, once smelled, would never be forgotten.

The inmates made hooch in recycled shampoo bottles, lotion bottles, black trash bags, old mayo jars, and gallon plastic jugs from the kitchen. Of course all these containers were clean and sterile, right?

The biggest season for home brew was Christmas and New Year's. The inmates had big parties. They made their own no-bake pies, bought cookies and candies, and tried to remind themselves of a better time at home. They policed their own so as not to get too rowdy. Sometimes it worked, sometimes it didn't.

One individual even made hooch while locked up in segregation. What nerve. He used an empty shampoo bottle and crammed all the ingredients into the small hole. The he secured the top and stuffed it into the neck of the toilet, pushed the button in on his warm water, and jammed it that way. The water ran continuously, thereby keeping his "works" warm and fermenting his hooch. After he was caught and photos were taken, he was prosecuted by the Bureau of Alcohol, Tobacco, and Firearms for brewing alcohol without a license. That charge was later reduced when he turned state's evidence against others for mail fraud, and he was transferred to KSP.

Weapons in a sock

These weapons could take several different forms. Inmates would put a lock in a sock, walk up behind someone, swing it, and POW! upside the head. The blow would split the head wide open; that usually required stitches. Such a gash usually bled a lot, too. Another variation was to put a can in a sock. Tuna, soup, mackerel, whatever. Same effect—split head, stitches. Talk about a splitting headache!

If they really wanted to do some damage, inmates put several cans in a laundry bag, swung it, and really hurt someone. I saw this happen once, and it split the victim's head wide open (twenty stitches) and knocked him out. He bled so much we thought he was going to bleed out and die, but my partner gloved up, grabbed a towel, and applied pressure till medical got there. Then it was a trip to the hospital. The inmate who attacked him went to SMU, and after his hole time was completed, he was transferred to maximum security at Eddyville, because retribution *was* promised. We later determined that the victim of the attack owed his attacker two snack cakes for a debt that hadn't been paid. Prison justice.

Regular weapons

With all the prison industries, there were a lot of tools in use. Although there was strict control of these tools, sometimes shit happens.

An inmate was scheduled for release. The day before, he was going through the checking-out process. Officers were going to different areas making sure he didn't have any library books overdue or games checked out, that he had his medical records in order, that he had three days' worth of meds to take with him. The inmate had to get his paperwork signed at each place he stopped. He was saying goodbye to old friends and coworkers. It was at the print shop where he had worked previously when it happened. Another inmate working there signed out a claw hammer. He then attacked the guy who was scheduled for release and beat his head in with it—crushed his skull, broke it open, and blood and brain matter came spewing out.

We never determined how many times he was hit, but it was *a lot*. He died in the print shop with his head split open and his brains coming out, one day away from parole. It was later determined that it was a lover's quarrel that had been festering for several days. Both men had had an affair with another inmate, and the one who killed his coworker was jealous. He was tried, convicted in state court, and given another life sentence.

Tobacco

Going smoke-free is not just for health reasons. It's also a matter of cleanliness—fewer matches on the ground, fewer butts to be picked up, no smoke film on the windows, less chance of a fire. The reasons are numerous, and the health saving should also be noted.

Most prisons were tobacco-free, including LLCC, starting in the spring of 2012. This means not only includes inmates, but staff also, and all forms of tobacco—cigarettes, cigars, chewing tobacco, snuff. No matter, it's all outlawed. There are still isolated cases of tobacco being smuggled into the prisons by staff and visitors, but it is harder for visitors than staff, since most areas are a long walk away from the parking lot. The staff just go into a staff restroom and do their thing. But on their thirty minute lunch break, many just go outside to their cars to enjoy their smokes.

Before tobacco was outlawed, cigarettes were just thrown on the ground, the janitors would sweep them up, pick out the butts, and take them back to their rooms. Here they would strip open the butts, take the tobacco out keep it, and buy or borrow rolling papers and reroll the tobacco to have "fresh" smokes. Talk about the ultimate recycle program. These recycled cigarette butts were known as "dead ducks."

Once they heard that smoking was going to be discontinued, the inmates started hoarding all the tobacco they could get and running a lucrative business until they ran out or smoked them all up. Those coming to seg often had their bibles prepped. (Maybe a special place in hell for those guys?) They removed the inside covers—front and back page—and secured some tobacco, matches, and rolling papers in there.

If they didn't have rolling papers, they had an ingenious way of getting them. They used the pages from the small pocket-sized bibles they were given in the chapel and *always* carried with them—seldom for the right reasons.

They also stuffed tobacco down the spine of their bibles or any school books they were allowed to have. There were many consequences for both the staff and inmates if they were caught.

For inmates, it could be anything from a written warning to hole time.

For staff, it could lead to termination from their job.

Chapter 13

Visits and Visitation—Family Day

The one constant that all inmates liked, wanted, and needed was visits. Once they got to prison and settled in a dorm, they saw their CTOs for one of the many items of paperwork they had to fill out, and that was their visiting list. No one could visit that was not on this list, and then it had to be verified and approved—verified that the visitors were not ex-cons, on probation or parole, or had a criminal history, or had been found with contraband on the prison premises. Any of the above had to be approved by the warden. Visitors were allowed to visit every other weekend according to the last digit in the inmate's number. If an inmate's number, i.e., 123456, ended in an even number, they could receive visitors on the weekends when the date was even, either Saturday or Sunday—but not both. On holidays, they were allowed an extra visit, first to come, first to leave. All visits were conducted this way when the visiting room reached full capacity of eighty-eight people. There were exceptions to this rule, such as when a family was traveling an extended distance. This distance was generally 250 miles or more. And these extended visits had to be approved in advance by the warden after the inmate applied through his CTO.

All visitors were searched before they were allowed to enter the visiting room. They were required to remove their coats, jackets, and sweaters, and remove all objects from their pockets. No hoodies were allowed. No skirts more then six inches above the knee. No midriff could show. Anything a visitor was allowed to bring in, such as any money—up to ten dollars in change for the vending machines—had to be in a clear see-through plastic purse or plastic zip-top baggy. This money was used to buy items for themselves and the inmate they were visiting. Visitors happily purchased all the goodies the inmate wanted or until the cash was gone, whichever came first. After all, it was not prison food, and the inmates only got it every weekend, unless they happened to be on meritorious status in a meritorious dorm, and they got the extra visit during the week with food brought in. The biggest sellers were hamburgers, sandwiches, coffee, chips, and sodas. Tobacco was not allowed, so they had to purchase cigarettes (four dollars per pack) out of the allotted ten dollars from a machine that was also inside the visiting room. This too would cease when the prison went tobacco-free.

Even the children were searched, but generally not as thoroughly. Often the parents would place contraband items on the children or in baby carriers or diaper bags to smuggle them in. If they got caught, they tried to duck the blame or pass it on—I didn't know it was in there, I checked it before we left home, and they must have put that in there. Or someone else put it in there. But their visits were then denied for that week, and a report was forwarded to the warden for final determination. A lot of small contraband items were placed in the kids' socks, underwear, or hidden in their crotch area, and later retrieved in the restroom. The worst of the bunch were the parents who placed items in babies' diapers, because these were never checked. Small balloons of dope were easy to hide and retrieve later in the restroom on the way to the visiting room, under the guise of changing the baby's diapers. The contraband was then washed and passed to the inmate with a kiss. The inmate would swallow the small balloon and it would later come to pass, so to speak.

Sometimes the visitors would secret contraband items on themselves, in their bra areas, crotch areas, or even inside themselves, and then retrieve them in the bathroom. Even prescription pills and bottles were used, the most common being the gel type pills that could be opened. The original medication was dumped and replaced with coke or heroin. But the visitors were restricted to only one dose of medication for the allotted time of the visit, one or two pills maximum.

Once inside the visiting room, visitors were assigned tables that corresponded to the number of visitors, with a max of four per table, unless a small child or two sat on an adult's lap, inmates excluded. Even when the visitor went to the restroom, if there was no other adult, they had to take the child or children with them. *No* kids remained with the inmates . . . period. After all, this was a prison with convicted sex offenders.

And no more than three restroom visits were allowed, or the visit was terminated. The reason for this was that many nature calls could be used for other than intended purposes. But so could one or two.

The length of visits was also controlled. When it was not crowded and the weather was nice, the inmates could choose to either go outside and sit at picnic tables or stay inside. This allowed for more visitors during the summer months. Generally visits were a minimum of thirty minutes when the visiting room was at full capacity. The maximum was open, as long as there was no waiting list. But visits generally two hours.

When the visiting room reached full capacity of eighty-eight (inside), it was first in, first out. It was hard to manage, but the only way was to log in the arrival time and table size so the visits could be as equal as possible. The holiday time was the worst because everyone wants to visit and stay as long as possible. I've seen visits terminated after thirty minutes because of a waiting list and the number of visitors waiting. Thanksgiving and Christmas were the worst. I've seen parents and inmates cry because they had their visits cut short. The mantra was "Why me?" and "Can't I please stay longer?" Visitors offered money and other incentives so the officers would let them stay longer, but even the visitors knew who came first and whose turn it was next to leave. The stress affected the officers working also.

Eventually the visitors figured out when the best time to arrive was. They knew that count was scheduled at approximately noon, and there was no inmate or visitor movement thirty minutes prior to that, or no movement until count cleared, generally about thirty minutes. So if they arrived forty-five minutes to an hour ahead of count, they could be safe in a longer visit through count time.

The visiting room was equipped with many video cameras and monitors, and everything was recorded in case it was needed later if someone was accused of trying to pass something. If there were any immediate questions, the tape could be reviewed by a supervisor immediately, and the appropriate action taken, such as termination of a visit or taking the inmate straight to segregation. No physical contact was allowed except for a brief hug and kiss upon arrival and departure. But there were a lot of "footsie" games played under the table. It reminded me of teenagers in love.

Meritorious visits were an extra perk for the "better" inmates living in 7D and 7E, the honor dorms. When they had their extra weekday visits, their visitors were allowed to bring in fast food items from outsides sources. At one time they were allowed to bring in such items as steaks, baked potatoes, salads, and bloomin' style onions. These were discontinued because visitors went overboard and created a mess. These items were replaced with pizzas, burgers, and sub sandwiches, all the usual fast food fare, and they brought it in in quantity.

I saw one inmate, a rather large fellow, devour a complete large pizza himself. His three family members shared a medium pizza and some burgers.

As a whole, most visitors were nice and polite and understood the enormous and taxing job the officers had to perform, and they accepted it and knew we were being firm, fair, and consistent. That's all they wanted.

Chapter 14

JUSTICE IN PRISON

One of the processes inside the prison system is called court call. When an inmate commits an infraction of the rules and gets caught, it's up to the officer who caught him to determine what he or she is going to do. It could range from a talking to or doing a write-up, or, if it's severe enough, the inmate is taken straight to the hole, with the captain's office approval. In this case, your "house" is packed up and inventoried for you. A write-up is more serious because it goes into the inmate's permanent record and then is there when they appear before the parole board, which could affect their release.

When an inmate is given a write-up, he is then required to appear before the adjustment committee, usually consisting of a lieutenant or captain. The penalty can range from dismissal to going to segregation or loss of good time, the time earned toward early release. Some other penalties were loss of privileges, i.e., canteen, phone restriction, recreation area, or gym restriction, depending on the write-up. One could even lose canteen privileges except for hygiene items and stamps, etc. Going to the hole also depended on several factors. If the infraction was serious, you would go straight to the hole, or it can be delayed, and you go on the waiting list until there is room in seg. Sometimes this waiting list can grow to up to ten or twelve people. When cells became available, the waiting list goes into effect. The SMU supervisor then calls the appropriate dorm and the dorm officer brings the inmates up from the yard to start their time in seg. Stays in seg ranged from fifteen days to years. Yes, years! But usually after one year in seg with still more time to serve, the inmates are transferred, usually to the maximum security prison KSP in Eddyville.

When an inmate goes to court call, he is also given the opportunity to be represented by legal counsel. This "legal eagle" is another inmate who has some legal experience or is trained in the prison system for this function. They often advise their "clients" on their best options and plead for a reduced sentence, or they bring out mitigating circumstances to try to get their client off. One inmate who did this was sharp as a tack, and when he made parole he got a job in Louisville working as a paralegal clerk in a downtown law firm. The counselors always did a good job regardless of the person they were defending or his crime. And the good ones were always in great demand doing this or helping in the law library doing research on their cases or assisting in someone else's case. The good ones were also in such high demand they had to go on a rotation basis for seg. This kept one person from getting burned out on cases and allowed them to work on their own cases, and take a little time off.

Chapter 15

LOCAL SUPERMARKET

The inmate canteen is the place where inmates spend their "money." The money they receive either comes from their prison jobs. They get paid only once a month, usually the last day, and the money is posted to their numbers accounts. Their time is kept by the officers for whom they work; i.e., records for all dorm workers such as janitors, bathroom cleaners, window washers, sidewalk sweepers, etc., are kept by the dorm officer. The inmates check in before they start and after they complete their jobs so they can be checked off. Sometimes an inmate's friends or family will send them some money, and some receive government checks, like social security or disability or retirement checks, that are also deposited in their accounts. If they have no family to get these checks, they are sent to the prison. Some like to control the money so they ask for the checks to be sent to them. Then their caseworker will send money to their families.

The money they spend, up to fifty dollars per week, with exceptions, such as TVs, Walkmans, etc., buys them groceries, candies, snacks, etc., and all hygiene items.

They must also buy their writing materials and stamps (another form of money on the yard). They buy *a lot* of noodles, cookies, snak (sic) cakes, fruit, and potatoes. Just like going shopping at their local supermarket, they have to manage their "cash" flow. They must fill out a "shopping list" and present it at the window of the canteen along with their ID card. They are given a total of money available to them and all items purchased are deducted from that total. This prevents them from shopping with someone else's ID. Since the inmates are only allowed to store a certain amount of food in their cells, they rented space in someone else's cell. The only problem with this is if they get shaken down and inspected, they must have a receipt for all their purchases. If not, the items are confiscated and they receive a write-up for unauthorized canteen, and the debt does not go away. Debts never do in prison. They even follow you when you go from one prison to another. Cons have connections everywhere, and debts are bought and sold through the mail.

The canteen is shared on a rotating basis. Mondays, it's Dorm 7A, Tuesdays, 7B, etc., until Friday. This always rotates . . . so the next week will start with 7B, etc. Once the line runs down to less than ten people, it is opened to the next dorm regardless of day. On Saturday it's open to anyone.

The canteen is a very lucrative business that's not part of the prison system. They make more than $2.5 million a year because this is the only place the inmates have to spend their money. After all, like the old song says, "I owe my soul to the company store." The prison does make a percentage of sales, based on the vendor's contract. After all, the state supplies the building, computers, utilities, and some manpower to help work there—inmate workers, such as truck unloaders, stockers, order fillers. The contract is open for bids when it expires. It all goes through the state bidding system.

Chapter 16

PRISON IN A PRISON

Segregation. The Hole. SMU. Dodge City. Solitary. Lock-up.
These were the terms that the officers and inmates used when they talked about segregation. And this where *the* most colorful stories came from. Although there are many that can't be told, here are some that really stay on my mind.

When someone came to SMU, it could have been for several different reasons; therefore, we had several different colored clothes to distinguish them and to identify their status.

Red clothes

Death row inmates wear red. Although we did not house them on a regular basis, occasionally we had them. These inmates were kept totally apart from all others—no contact at all, and any time they were out of their cells, they wore handcuffs and leg shackles and were escorted by two officers and one supervisor.

They were given the highest security level any time they had to be moved. No other inmates could be in the immediate area. If they had to come or go down the walkway, the yard was usually closed or the walk was totally closed. It depended upon the inmate being transported, but the rule was total isolation.

James R. Palmer

Yellow clothes
Yellow was for inmates on the yard who decided to "check in" to SMU for personal reasons, such as fear for their life. They might be informants who were found out (a snitch), and so decided to check in using protective custody (PC) as a means to let thing cool down. We called these guys prison chickens (PC). They might have accumulated some debts they could not pay, and checking in was a way to delay that debt until they could call or write home and have some money sent in to their account. (*Remember all calls are subject to be monitored.*) After release, they could go to the inmate commissary to purchase some goodies or stamps to pay that debt off, with interest. But once an inmate gets a reputation of checking in or being PC, it follows him like a trail of bad stink, even from prison to prison. And it never leaves, no matter where the inmate goes or what excuses or stories they told to other inmates. An inmate also might be ordered by a gang leader to check in with the purpose to conduct a beat down on someone.

Green clothes
This color was used by all other inmates when they came to "reside" in SMU. They could come from court call, off the waiting list, from another prison due to over crowding, or from a prison that did not have a segregation unit.

Blue clothes
This color was worn by inmates who came to us from another prison due to various reasons such as the intake unit at RCC, before inmates got assigned to a particular prison, or from another prison until they transferred to us or another prison.

Shoes
After we changed their clothes to the correct color code, we also had to change their shoes because the inmates liked to remove the heels from their boots, hollow them out, and stuff them with . . . tobacco or drugs or things that could be used as weapons. So we gave them all orange slip-on tennis shoes and a pair of sandals. We

called the shoes "air wardens"—always trying to inject a little humor into a trying situation.

Smuggling

When an inmate arrived in SMU for whatever reason, he was allowed to keep certain items, such as legal paperwork and certain books for reference. But tobacco was not one of them, so smuggling tobacco was a constant battle. They used books by separating the binding from the book and packing it with tobacco and rolling papers and a few match heads. One match head could be split in two to make two matches.

They used the inside covers of books, especially the back inside of bibles. They would carefully peel away the paper, pack it with tobacco and the rest of the fixin's to roll 'em. The church groups that visited the prison usually brought in the small pocket bibles. The inmates liked them a lot because the pages of the bible were very similar to regular rolling papers. Since they were allowed bibles in segregation, they had an almost endless supply of papers. Now all they needed was the tobacco.

Many times they just made a "butt plug" that contained everything they needed. It was secreted in their butt (thus butt plug), and when they got to their cell, they retrieved it, rolled one, and returned it to its hiding place. Ahh, what flavor that must have been! When an inmate smoked in segregation, it was evident, as the smell and smoke lingered a long time. When the officers patrolled the wings every fifteen minutes, it was noticeable, and sometimes easy to follow. Then we would do a cell search with a complete strip search and usually find the contraband. The inmate would get another write-up and get an extra thirty days in the hole.

As mentioned before, a good partner was hard to find. I had one in segregation. His nickname was M.O. He always had our back. He loved to work the control center. He was very meticulous in his logs and record keeping. And wherever we went, he was always listening and watching. Segregation had speakers and cameras everywhere, and he controlled all of them. We knew he was listening and watching us even when we were in the cells. Even when we were not in the cells, M.O. would randomly select cells and listen to conversation. The speakers were always on and M.O. was always taking notes. (Probably still has them.) I think this is where the saying "if walls could talk" came from.

We had hand signals and signs, so most of the time we didn't need to talk. Voices and noises traveled well and echoed a lot. So our hand and eye signals worked great. We heard a lot, found out a lot, and learned a lot. And we passed a lot on to IA.

Then there was the "dirty old man." This old man was probably the nastiest we ever had in segregation. He would wipe his feces on the walls, his clothes, floor, bed, and bedding. When that happened, we had to move him to another cell across the hall from his. That meant taking up two cells for one person, so his old one could be cleaned and sanitized. The inmate janitors had this responsibility, and they also took all health precautions—gloves, masks, paper suits, booties, and masks. We kept track of everything we used to clean his cell so he would be billed for it. He had an extensive bill, but not all of it was paid before he served out his time. He even flushed his clothes down the toilet and stopped up the pipes. Once they had to be dug up by maintenance and cleaned out. Eventually he was handcuffed, shackled, and left to lie on his cold steel bed with no sheets blankets or clothes, buck naked. He never complained or bitched about it, but he stayed nasty. Each time we opened his food tray slot to feed him—and we had to feed him—he would hobble over and try to spit on us. He usually just took his food tray and threw it either on the walls and ceiling or at us. So we changed his menu. We had the kitchen take the same items they were feeding the inmates on the yard, add some flour and an egg blend, and bake it into a loaf, and he was served that. We called it SEG LOAF. It was nutritious, filling and . . . bland. He threw that too for awhile but it didn't stick to anything. It ended up like crumbled bread. Eventually he got hungry. After months of living like this, he realized he was not going to win and changed his ways, and eventually made it out to the dorms. But while it lasted, he was nasty.

There was Crazy D. He had about a fourth grade education, was out there in the ozone somewhere. He was such a problem child that he was rotated every ninety days from prison to different prison, and no one enjoyed it when he arrived because they knew what they were in for. He was usually a jovial guy but when he got *that* look in his eye, we knew it was coming. He was only about five foot nine and 145 pounds, but when his adrenaline was pumping and his eyes glassed over, it was like he was Superman on steroids. I was involved once when it took seven of us to control him and get him off one officer—what a fight! But give him some crayons and some paper to color on and he was happy.

I was working on a Thanksgiving Day with officer M.O. It was to be my last patrol of the day before shift change. Time was about 3:17 p.m. As I passed a cell in A wing upper, I looked in the cell door window. There was inmate Charlie, who had his bed sheet threaded through his air vent and tied around his neck. I ran down to the control center and hollered to M.O., "Give me the cut down knife, Charlie is hanging himself." He tossed me the knife and I ran back upstairs with two lieutenants following me. We got to his door, M.O. opened it, the lieutenants grabbed his legs and lifted him, and I cut his sheets down. We then put him on suicide watch, which consisted of bare cell, no mattress no pillow, sheets or blankets, with just a nontearable gown. We did our paperwork and reports and still made it out on time at the end of our shift twenty-five minutes later. I was off the next two days, and when I returned, I saw inmate Charlie still on suicide watch. He stopped me and said he didn't remember anything about what happened, but said, "Thanks for saving my sorry ass."

There were many suicide attempts in seg. Although items such as razors were strictly controlled, the inmates were very inventive. They used combs, the plastic sporks they were given (combination spoon and fork—no knives), and paper clips. They used whatever they had. The ones who wore glasses tried using the arms on their glasses. They broke the glass in their lenses and tried to use that to cut themselves. The glass was thick and caused deep slashes. They broke their plastic cups and used the jagged edges. They would bust their plastic food trays to get jagged plastic. Then we would switch to styrofoam cups and trays. When they wanted to try, there was nothing they wouldn't use. Someone took out the metal air vents in the mattress and used them to cut himself. Although no one ever succeeded, some made big bloody messes, and some came awfully close.

But most used the suicide ruse for attention. If they wanted to kill themselves, they could, but they would usually cut themselves across the wrist, making several small cuts, rather than big long cuts going up the arms along major arteries.

Each cell has a sprinkler system head it in. This is in case the concrete walls, ceilings, concrete floor, steel bunk, and stainless steel sink catch fire. Oh, yeah, they do have blankets and sheets and paper and other items they can burn. And they have been known to smuggle in matches. Or contraband sometimes is sent in in their food trays from the kitchen. When someone is expecting something, the word is passed and whoever gets it finds ways to pass it, especially when there is outside rec. They hide it and word is passed; we try to listen and watch—again the game of cat and mouse. But one inmate thought he would see if the sprinkler heads really did work. (They do.) He knocked the head off his sprinkler with his food tray. Well, all the water that had been in the steel pipes for years came spewing out, rusty colored, cold, and under *extreme* pressure. The shut-off valve is located outside for safety reasons, so the water gushed like a sideways volcano. The opening under the door is about a half inch. The water got knee deep before it was shut off. The cells are only eleven by nine feet. He got wet. Really wet. And cold. But he did clean the pipes for us. And got a write-up for destruction of state property, which he paid for.

When unruly inmates had to be restrained for periods of time, we used a restraint chair. It was a padded seat on a thirty degree angle, which made it hard to stand up, and the inmate was strapped in a chair around the wrists, ankles, and shoulders. Restraint could be extended for up to three hours, and these inmates were always checked by medical. Once secured, the chairs could not be moved. The inmates could rock them but not tip them over or roll them. We secured a spit hood over the heads of those who tried to spit on us. It was like a fishnet hood that fitted over the head. It did not cut off air circulation, but had an elastic closure, and it was see-through, uncomfortable but not confining. After spending time in the chair, the inmate usually calmed down enough to be released back to his cell where he had to begin earning back what he'd lost—mattress sheets, blankets, and clothes.

Long stays in seg worked on their minds. If an inmate didn't keep his mind occupied by reading, writing letters, doing puzzle books, etc., anything to keep their minds sharp, they did deteriorate mentally, especially with longer stays. They also slept—a lot. After all, they had no TV or radios, and sitting in a cell all day looking out a two inch by three foot window got boring too. All they had in the cell was a steel bunk with mattress, an eighteen-inch square table bolted to the wall, and a combination sink and toilet, also bolted to the floor and wall.

Talking to their neighbor in the next cell got old too, and talking in their cells echoed a lot and kept everyone awake. So much for peace and quiet.

So at the end of a long day, the end of another shift, we just wanted to be sure that we all did our jobs and accomplished the same thing—protected the public, guarded our charges, and got home to our families safe and sound.

One good thing about working in seg is we got *a lot* of exercise. There were two sets of stairs, eight steps to each set for each wing, and we did our patrols every fifteen minutes, all day—plus all the extra trips up and down for pill call; feeding; retrieving food trays after meals; getting inmates out for medical, to see the CTO or UA; getting them out and returning them to and from rec. or phone calls, which had to be scheduled and only one per week. It kept us going, and we did a lot of walking.

Chapter 17

CELL ENTRIES FOR STUBBORN CONVICTS

While most of the cell entries take place in segregation, there are some that occasionally happen in the dorms. These are performed when inmates don't comply to come out of their cell for various reasons. They have hidden contraband or they just want to fight, or they got off their meds and think that people are out to harm them or get at them. They see things and hear voices. Sometimes the entries are used as a diversion for something or someone else that's about to happen. That person is "paid" to cause a scene or ruckus to divert the attention of the officers to that area. That's why there are response teams assigned, so not everyone responds to the trouble area that's called out. Never use all your resources in one area, and watch all other areas closely to see what else is going on.

The cell entry teams that respond to SMU are more specialized. They are always a team of five that has more specialized training and a non-SMU supervisor. Another person is always assigned to camera duty, as all cell entries *must* be filmed. This is for the protection of the staff and inmate, in case someone gets injured or the inmate files a lawsuit, as they usually do.

The special training we all had to go through was the same as what we meted out.

The stun shield is a Plexiglas shield equipped with stun capabilities of fifty thousand volts. To use it, we had to go through feeling what it felt like, in case it ever went to court and we were asked if we knew what it felt like. Yeah, we did. The same with the pepper spray. We all had to get a dose of that in the face and eyes. So we knew. The stun shield was controlled by a toggle thumb switch, and it was only used if the person on the receiving end became combative and tried to fight. It was also used to protect staff. The inmates didn't care and they used all the tricks they could muster up. They would squirt shampoo or lotion on the floor so when the team opened the door to their cell and rushed in, they had no footing and it was slip slidin' away. Or they covered themselves with the lotion or shampoo so we couldn't get a good grip on them. Or they would hold their mattress in front of them to stop the stun shield. But each person on the entry team had a specific role. First in was the shield man. His job was to contain and pin the inmate to the bed, wall, or floor. The inmate was always asked to comply and lay on the bed, but they didn't always comply. The second person in took control of the right arm, the third took the left arm, the fourth had the right leg, and the fifth in had the left leg.

Each person had a job, and it was done in a professional manner and in silence. That was because the only person talking was the supervisor, who was always in control, giving orders and directions. The camera was always running to record the event in case of *any* allegations of wrongdoing. After each cell entry, the inmate was examined by medical to insure there were no injuries either to staff or inmate.

Sometimes when an inmate tried to commit suicide by cutting himself, he would be covered in blood and there would be blood all over the floor. Very gory scenes. One of the first instincts of the officers was to rush in and try to save that person. That's what we we're trained to do—protect and serve. But we had to stay back, observe, and just remember what was going on for the reports to be filed later. But we also had to take all the universal precautions in case they had any communicable diseases, such as HIV, AIDS, or hepatitis. We suited up in protective gowns; we wore knee pads, elbow pads, riot helmets with face shields, and protective gloves. After all, we didn't want to get hurt or take anything home to our families, and we didn't always know what diseases they had. Medical always said, "If you go in. I would dress up." That way they never violated the HIPAA laws.

Some inmates became so unruly they had to secured and strapped down to a bed in a cell. These were usually the ones who were off their meds and needed to be force medicated. It didn't happen often, but it did happen, and always under the orders of a medical doctor and nurse supervisor. They always continued to fight because, they insisted, they were okay, and nothing was wrong.

After the cell entries or extractions were over, everybody involved had to write reports and attend debriefings on what went right or wrong and what, if anything, we could do to make it better the next time. Unfortunately, there always was a next time.

While nobody liked to do cell entries or extractions because it was as dangerous for us as it was them, it was a necessary part of our duties, because someone could always get hurt. Luckily, not many did because of the care and demanding training we had—not to mention practice, practice, practice.

After it was all over, most of the inmates showed remorse and some even apologized. Until the next time.

Chapter 18

ASSAULTS ON STAFF AND INMATES

While assaults do happen in prison, most are committed inmate on inmate. However, there are some that do occur against staff. When an inmate has it in for a staff member, not much can be done to prevent an assault from happening. The best offense is a good defense. We are taught to be aware of our surroundings, to get a "feel" for the dorms, the convicts, and the yard. Listen to what the inmates talk about without getting in their conversations. Just listen. You would be surprised as to what you hear. A bit here, a piece there, and suddenly *something* comes together. Sometimes it's just a mood you feel. *Trust* that gut instinct—it's usually correct. Always let your partner(s) know where you are, just in case. Your partner is one of your best assets. But always know that response is close at hand, even though it may seem like a long time for them to get there.

When *it* happens, everything seems to go in slow motion. Pay attention to details and take a quick look around to see who's there as a possible witnesses or what might be a clue, such as a laundry bag with a can in it, or a lock in sock—whatever seems out of place or unusual at the time. Take mental notes and photos, until you can write it down.

I was assaulted three times, all while working in SMU, the most secure building in the prison. While we were usually under constant observation while in a wing (there were four of them), it's hard to see all at the same time. The good thing is having a working radio and being able to use it when necessary—and having a great partner in the control center.

One memorable day as I was picking up food trays and checking to see if the inmates wanted to go for outside recreation, I was getting ready to release them as we had done in the past after picking up their food trays. On this particular day two inmates wanted to get me for reasons unknown, and the ruse they used as they came out for rec was that they wanted to fight each other with me caught in the middle. I was able to grab my radio and call a signal seven, and defend myself. The other inmates were watching and cheering (not for me); they enjoyed it, even as short as it was. The first officer responded in less than ten seconds and the rest in less than two minutes. What a sight to see them all respond! My adrenaline was pumping, I was shaking and breathing hard, but after the paperwork was done, I went back to my assigned tasks. I finished picking up food trays and getting the other inmates out for recreation, continuing as if nothing happened. *Never* let them see that you are scared or worried. The inmates will feed on it, and then they will try to use it to their advantage.

It's not always the physical assaults that are dangerous. Some inmates make "cocktails" concocted from urine, blood, vomit, feces, and spit, then throw them at us. Usually we don't know it's coming, so it's hard to avoid. But after all is said and done, it's another charge against them, usually outside charges for assault on a peace officer, with more time added to their sentence. The scary part is, what kind of diseases are they carrying and possibly passing on to us and our families?

When an inmate assaults a staff, there are a lot of ramifications that follow. The inmate will *always* lose the battle. Oh, he may get his licks in, but so will the officers. You know, for every action there is a reaction. And when the group responds, *we* never lose.

Sometimes the inmates even gets transferred to another prison, usually farther from home, which puts an undue hardship on the families as the travel requirements are now harder and more expensive for them. And then the inmates blame the DOC for causing the hardship, rather then telling their families what they did.

The same goes when they attack each other. Other than the assaults mentioned above, some of the worst happened as they just walked the yard.

Everyone minds their own business when one inmate walks up to another on the walkway and just sucker punches the other. It's completely unexpected and often ugly. These attacks usually only lasted several punches with the so-called winner throwing the first one. But they both end up going to seg until it gets sorted out.

Chapter 19

STRANGE (BED) FELLOWS

While this chapter covers some of the oddities, it by no means covers them all.

We had several people who were going through the "change of life," so to speak. They were in the transformation from male to female and thus they couldn't be housed in the female prison, so we got them. After all, they were still males. Some had gone so far as to have implants or taken hormone shots to enhance themselves above the waist but they still had the male anatomy as well. We had to clothe them, so occasionally we had to get such items as sport bras. They were usually the hit of the dorms t and had to be watched more closely. They were propositioned quite often, and most made a decent living accepting the offers.

Their crimes usually were committing robberies and burglaries, trying to get the money to continue or finish their transformation from one sex to another. Some even had photos of themselves dressed up, and they sure put up a good front, from the hair to the makeup to their clothes. Of course that was before they came to prison. Once they were locked up, they still tried to continue with their beauty ways. Some of the tricks of the trade were using pool cue chalk as eyeliner. A different colored drawing pencil was another trick for eyeliner or lipstick or to outline their lips, or as rouge to color their cheeks. It worked well for short periods of time, but sweating or rain usually took care of that. Then they had to repowder their noses.

Paper clips were used for earrings as were homemade items fashioned from tin foil that came with some food items. Some even used the straw ends of brooms to keep their ears from closing up. They tried to get the straw from new brooms, but that was not always possible. Necessity was the mother of invention and some even cleaned up pretty good. To some of the inmates they were nines on a scale of ten. Love is found in the strangest places.

Some of these hook-ups continued even after one or both left prison; some flourished, some didn't. And to some, it was just a matter of convenience.

One inmate had a severe facial deformity that was so bad it looked like it straight out of Hollywood horror movie. He couldn't eat or drink normally. When he ate, he had to scrape his food from his tray into his mouth and then chew what he could.

To drink he used a large syringe to squirt his water or juice into his mouth. He always carried at least two rags with him because he drooled so much because he had a hard time swallowing. The other inmates were always harassing or teasing him, making fun of him, so he got to eat his meals fifteen minutes ahead of everyone else. Usually he ate alone, most often standing in the janitor's closet. Then it was back to his room, where he spent most of his time. His deformity was due to an attempted suicide with a shotgun, gone bad at the last second. He tried to change his mind just as he pulled the trigger. A half miss . . . or a half hit?

Chapter 20

MONEYMAKERS

As with most aspects of life, there are money-making opportunities everywhere, even in prison. Not all jobs in prison are sanctioned or state sponsored, but they go on with the knowledge of staff and officials alike. They are often overlooked as long they are not openly blatant and not illegal.

Not all laundry is done in the prison laundry for free. If you want your clothes done quickly with the personal touch, it costs you. There are four washers and dryers in each dorm, two of each for every two wings, and a laundry man assigned to each. It is supposed to be free, but the going rate is one pack of cigarettes per laundry bundle. For this you get your clothes washed, dried, and folded neatly and delivered to your door. Of course you have to supply the soap powder and dryer sheets if you want good smelling, static-free clothes. You want them pressed? Yeah, that costs extra too.

There are artists in prison who make greeting cards, and a pretty good living. Colored pencils are used. Then when they get too small for the artists to use, they "recycle" them to the ones who will use them as eyeliner, etc. Inmates smuggle thicker paper, almost the same as a regular greeting cards, out of the print shop. It is then bought by the artists, who in turn make the cards. If you need a card for a birthday, anniversary, missing you, Valentine's Day, Christmas, or whatever the occasion, you go see the artist. He can even personalize the inside of the card if you wish. If you're not poetic, he will be. Or there is a poet in the dorm somewhere, and the cost is only one pack for two cards, which also come with homemade envelopes. Sorry, you provide the stamps. (But for a price, to be paid later, they could also be provided.)

For the holidays, the prices go up somewhat because of the demand for more cards for Thanksgiving, Christmas, and New Year's. And order early—you don't want to miss a special occasion. They are cheaper than the cards at the inmate canteen. The only thing missing is the bar code on the back!

Prison clothes are one size fits nobody! Most just wear them. Those who have a fashion sense want tailored, or at least better fitting, clothes. They get them done by a "tailor" in the dorms. Just needle and thread, no machine work, and the cost is one pack per pair of pants or shirt that is altered. The job is done in a timely manner and delivered to you when complete.

Don't like the food in the chow hall? Can't cook? There is always someone who can. All you have to do is provide the groceries and they'll whip up something for you to eat. But get enough for two because your fee is feeding the cook also.

Need a Christmas present for your kid? How about a home made jewelry box? Or a catch-all box for your son's change or your daughter's, wife's, or mother's trinkets? A jewelry box? Custom made from Popsicle sticks or matches or both. There are some very good works produced by inmates. The cost is dependent upon the size and intricacy of the piece being constructed. But be sure to order in time for mailing home.

Haircuts are also provided free of charge to all prisoners. However, if you don't want the standard buzz cut, and want instead a nice neat trim and good style, its going to cost you. A pack per haircut. And you have to have an appointment made on your dorm's day.

If you don't have any cigarettes to trade, you can also do a trade in stamps or food, but when the prison goes tobacco-free, the new prices will be in stamps or food items. Snack cakes sure are a big hit in prison, and packages of noodles. They can be very creative with what they have.

Chapter 21

Time Winds Down

The end of your time in prison can come in several different ways.

Serve out

The inmate can serve out his sentence. That means he has completed his time and paid his or her debt to society and is free to go. Sometimes the release is with restrictions and sometimes not, but the name, ex-felon, will always stick. When applying for jobs, you are usually asked if you have ever been convicted of a crime. Answer yes and you probably won't get an interview. Answer no, and if they check, they'll find out you lied and you won't get the job. Catch 22.

That's why it's so hard for ex-cons to get a job.

Parole

The inmate can make parole. This is usually done by serving a certain portion of the time you were given in court. It can range from a minimum of one year up, again depending on the time given and the crime committed.

For violent crimes, there is a minimum of 85 percent. This means on a twenty-year sentence, you must serve seventeen years before you can get parole. It *does not* mean automatic parole, just eligibility after seventeen years. There are always restrictions attached to parole. Some are few and some are quite lengthy, and the parolee usually has to pay a fee to the state through his PO, each month.

This fee usually goes into a fund for the families of victims of certain crimes.

Shock probation

This type of release is usually granted to a person who has committed a lesser crime but receives a sentence greater than one year. It must not be a violent crime, and the person must be a first offender. The inmate must apply to the judge to receive this and then only after ninety days. It is not automatic, and it depends on the inmate's behavior and the type of crime committed. The families are usually contacted and have a chance to give input.

Death

Yes, death does also come to prison. It comes in many ways, just like outside of prison. Old age, natural causes, heart attacks, or disease, such as AIDS, hepatitis, or cirrhosis of the liver.

Those who die in a prison hospital or a civilian hospital and have a family to claim the body are usually buried in the family plot or the local cemetery.

Then there are those who die in prison or a civilian hospital while under the care of the state prison system. If they have no family to claim them or the family refuses to take care of the burial, they are then buried on state property, usually hidden out of the way in a nondescript area of prison property. They have a name for this place, and it's usually something like "chicken hill" or "free man's land" or "no man's land." Either way, it is *the* final resting place.

Epilogue

Quitting Time

And now comes the shift change. Time to take a deep breath, start to unwind, and relax a little. Go home and see our families. Give the oncoming officers a briefing as to what kind of day we had, and maybe what they can expect during their shift.

But with all said and done, as we gathered outside the front doors, we had still had to relate to each other what it was like that day, especially if we had any codes or signals.

One thing we were all grateful and happy for we were all going home . . . safe.

And we mostly had in the back of our minds the question, *Was I firm—fair—consistent?*